che on my mind

margaret randall

Duke University Press   Durham and London   2013

© 2013 Duke University Press. All rights reserved.
Printed in the United States of America on acid-free paper ∞
Designed by Courtney Leigh Baker. Typeset in Minion Pro
by Tseng Information Systems, Inc.
Library of Congress Cataloging-in-Publication Data
Randall, Margaret, 1936–
Che on my mind / Margaret Randall.
pages cm
Includes bibliographical references.
ISBN 978-0-8223-5578-6 (cloth : alk. paper)
ISBN 978-0-8223-5592-2 (pbk. : alk. paper)
1. Guevara, Che, 1928–1967. 2. Guerrillas—Latin America—
Biography. 3. Revolutionaries—Latin America—Biography.
I. Title.
F2849.22.G85R35 2013
980.03′5092—dc23
[B]
2013013826

This book is for Roxanne Dunbar-Ortíz
with thanks, always, for conversations that matter

contents   *acknowledgments* ⋆ ix

acknowledgments

A lifetime of reading, conversations, emotion, and firsthand experience has gone into this book. Influences and people are too numerous to mention, or even remember at this point in my life. During the writing itself, I have been grateful to Mark Behr, John Beverley, Louis Bickford, Sarah Brooks, Barbara Byers, Sabra Moore, Wolfram Morales, V. B. Price, Gregory Randall, Tineke Ritmeester, Greg Ruggiero, Robert Schweitzer, Susan Sherman, and Richard Vargas for important input and discussion. I also deeply appreciate my editor at Duke University Press, Gisela Fosado, and the two anonymous readers whose comments and suggestions enriched the text.

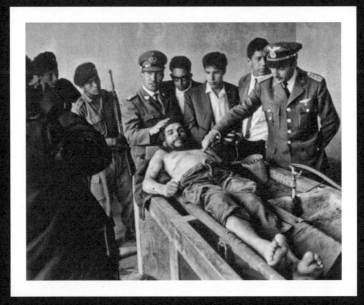

Che dead, surrounded by his
captors, schoolhouse, Vallegrande,
Bolivia, October 9, 1967. Photo by
Freddy Alborta.

chapter one
a death that leads us back to life

Ernesto Che Guevara occupies a place in our emotional iconography unsurpassed by anyone with the exception of Buddha, Mohammed, Marx, Mary, or Jesus of Nazareth. Still contemporary—his death at the age of thirty-nine isn't yet half a century behind us—he is a figure revered in equal measure by both convinced revolutionaries and apolitical youth at the farthest reaches of our planet. All see in him a symbol of nonconformity and resistance. And as with so many humans we've embalmed in myth, scholars and those who don't think past the image, devotees and detractors alike, tend to ignore a more nuanced view of the man.

I am old enough to remember the world in which he lived. I was part of that world, and it remains a part of me. This won't be a political or economic treatise, except where that sort of analysis strengthens my observations. It is a poet's reminiscence of an era and of the figure who best exemplifies that era. These musings may also help us rethink revolutionary change and see how a reexamination of history may point to more productive ways of achieving that change.

This is the story of how Che haunts me. I call it *Che on My Mind*, mimicking the old Hoagy Carmichael and Stewart Gorrell tune

"Georgia on My Mind." It's that spirit and wandering rhythm I wish to evoke: moving in one direction and then another, exploring this texture or that, giving free rein to memory and to a consciousness Che helped to shape.

In these notes I want to remember that Guevara was first and foremost extraordinarily human. He felt the pain of others deeply and subverted every social hypocrisy, every greed-based corporate crime and mean-spirited exploitation. Without doubt, the quality he embodied that made him beloved by millions was his unerring capacity to be who he said he was. In Che, words and actions were one. What he did was consistent with what he said. In a world where corporate crime, governmental sleight of hand, and the deterioration of moral values are every day more evident and endemic, the man's principles shine.

Because the energy of his internationalism burns as hot now as when he was alive, Che's image moves beyond easy metaphor. His myth has remained alive in disparate cultures. That myth, however, has been woven by friend and foe alike. Che's image, words, values, intentions, successes, and failures have all been shaped to symbolize that which he most deeply abhorred as well as that for which he died.

The most famous image of Che in life, the photograph of him wearing a black beret with the single star and looking into the future, was snapped by chance on March 5, 1960. A Belgian freighter, Le Coubre, had exploded in the Havana harbor, killing eighty Cubans. Che appeared at the mass funeral, and when he stepped to the edge of the speaker's platform, Alberto "Korda" Díaz snapped two consecutive 35 mm frames. This iconic image has circled the globe; it has been featured on posters, clothing, and even in an advertisement for Smirnoff vodka.[1]

Almost forty-five years after his assassination, some still remember his sacrifice with pride or nostalgia, others would say "Good riddance," and many more have only the vaguest notion of who he was—or no notion at all. Yet from the grotesquery of his severed hands, preserved in a Cuban crypt; through the hundreds of biographies, treatises, and poems written to or about him; to a million portraits spray-painted on walls and cheap T-shirts with his immediately recognizable visage sold in bazaars from Cairo to Siem Riep and Naples to his own Rosario, Argentina, Che is a name known in every language on earth.

The way he acquired that name is worth a few lines. In Ernesto Guevara's country of origin the brief syllable is broadly applied to all young males, much the same way Buddy or Dude or some other generic might be used in English. As a young man in Argentina, Guevara was Ernesto or Ernestito: the oldest son whose name echoed his father's. Occasionally and at different periods during his childhood or adolescence, he responded to a variety of nicknames. It wasn't until he arrived in Mexico and joined Fidel Castro and his group of Cuban exiles that he became Che: the Argentine. Meeting the man who would lead him to his destiny gave him the sobriquet that stuck, the one that would be inscribed in history. So Che denotes the foreign as well as the familiar. One of the twentieth century's most unique personalities assumed the commonest of verbal identities, one shared by hundreds of thousands in his native land. At the same time, once applied to him it took on a new and individualized meaning. In Che—the name as well as the man—the ordinary became extraordinary.

We may also coax out an additional layer of meaning from this name. Its Argentinean application to all males draws our attention to cultures—every culture I have known—in which the very terms *dude, guy, buddy, man, bro*, or their equivalents bring to mind a sort of macho stance, tolerated or even forgiven because "boys will be boys" and "men will be men." In English, all one has to do with the visual iconography is to remove the *C*; what remains is *he*: he, him, the male pronoun. We remain unconscious of the leap our eyes make as they subtract the initial letter. Implication lodges itself in our cells. It is through the multiple and contested narratives of public discourse that reality, thought, interpretation, and opinion constantly change, are made, unmade, and remade.[2] It is in this context that the name *Che* carries a distinctly masculine tone, one I will return to as I ponder the place of both man and myth in twentieth-century popular consciousness.

I never met Ernesto Guevara, but every so often, with an insistence as physical as spiritual, his memory draws me to revisit his life, ponder the attraction he exerts long past death, and read anew his writings and what others continue to write about him. My sources are mostly secondary, my intuitions those of a poet. I am mesmerized not by the man's power, which I often find to be exaggerated or hotheaded, but by his continued capacity to empower. I am moved more by his consistency and great generosity of spirit than by his sometimes-questionable political strategy or tactics.

I remember the moment of his death as vividly as if it were yesterday. October 9, 1967. Mexico City. A single mother, I had brought my ten-month-old firstborn to live in that city at the beginning of the decade. Now I also had a Mexican husband and two daughters. South of the border had become my home. The news came, impossible to believe at first but quickly and devastatingly confirmed, that the man my generation was counting on to lead Latin America's great movement for social change was dead. Young and rebellious myself at the time, I joined others who flooded the streets that night to paint "Che Vive" (Che Lives) on walls that had borne witness to struggle from the time of the Spanish conquest.

Three weeks later I traveled to the tiny island of Janitzio on beautiful Lake Pátzcuaro in the state of Michoacán. I was translating for a Canadian Film Board crew that was making a movie about Rufino Tamayo.[3] It was Mexico's Day of the Dead, and a silent procession of indigenous men and women wound their way through narrow lanes to the island's cemetery at the top of the hill.[4] These were Purépecha people, perhaps also Otomí and Nahua. On their shoulders they carried immense *ofrendas*, armatures of hardened bread dough adorned with painted flowers and birds. They would spend the night with their departed, picnicking at grave-sides, drinking and praying.

At that moment Che's assassination at the hands of my own country's Central Intelligence Agency (CIA) stood in for every death I had known. Witnessing the rituals of these indigenous poor, I thought of the Bolivians of the Altiplano for whom Che fought and died. Cultural devastation. Resignation and rebellion. The ugly residue of conquest. Mexico's elaborate ritual and Che's final effort in Bolivia became inextricably linked in my conscious-ness. Today, when I think of one, the others float to the forefront of my memory.

It would be years before I could begin to piece together how Che Guevara died. Were he and his two comrades ambushed at Que-brada del Churro or Quebrada del Yuro? Ñancahuazú or Mauricio? Did an enemy bullet incapacitate his M2, or did that even make a difference? Was he so doubled over with asthma, hunger, and exhaustion that he was unable to resist? Another member of the guerrilla force, one of the few who survived, describes his leader as weighing ninety pounds on that last day. Another portrays him dragging his rifle in the mud, without the strength to lift it off the ground.

At the moment of his capture did Che really say, "Don't shoot. I am Che Guevara: more useful to you alive than dead"? What of the mysterious young teacher some say brought him a last meal she'd cooked herself? Most men in that remote village oscillated between reactions of brutality and fear. A woman alone brought the doomed man sustenance and a few friendly words. What can we infer from this gender disparity among the villagers' responses when the mysterious enemy combatant suddenly appeared in their midst? The men were soldiers, firmly under the command of their superiors. Their meager paychecks demanded obedience to a chain of command. A few risked a human gesture; most mimicked a conqueror's stance. The lone woman was a teacher. In addition to her more compassionate instinct, she was probably also somewhat better educated than her neighbors.

What of the conversation Che—a teacher to the end—is rumored to have had with one of the young Bolivian soldiers guarding him, about a misspelled word on a piece of paper? And after his captors took him, wounded and with hands and feet bound, to the small schoolhouse at La Higuera, were his last words really "Shoot, coward, you are only killing a man"? All these incidents or presumed incidents, all these real or embroidered quotes, have been passed down from witnesses to friends or acquaintances as well as wending their way into the writing of utterly removed scribes, each with a particular interest to defend.

We do know that in the final effort to capture Guevara and the remaining rebels in his emaciated force, an extraordinarily cruel offensive was launched. Che was severely asthmatic, and for months all asthma medication and cortisone were removed from every hospital, pharmacy, and clinic over a vast area to prevent the possibility of the guerrillas attacking a dispensary and getting their hands on the precious remedies. Many of the Bolivian troops were replaced by US Rangers. The enemy outnumbered the guerrillas approximately three thousand to one. A handful of exhausted, hungry, sick revolutionaries were surrounded by battalions of well-trained well-armed soldiers with a single objective: to do away with the man who struck such fear in imperialism's heart.

Some of those soldiers treated their famous prisoner with respect; others taunted or battered him. One stole his last possessions—a dead combatant's watch he had promised to deliver to the man's family, his pipe, money, maps, a single hardboiled egg, and of course his diary.

Among those present was an official who called himself Capitán Ramos. This was Félix Rodríguez of the CIA. He subjected Guevara to a belittling interrogation, then took him outside the schoolhouse and propped him up so he could get someone to snap his picture with the guerrilla leader. Only after he had this personal memento did he order one of his underlings to carry out the execution that had already been decided at Langley and approved by Bolivian president René Barrientos. In subsequent years Rodríguez would repeat in self-serving detail his story of those moments with Che, embellishing it at every telling.

With their prize prey dead, the Bolivian military staged the tableaux that imprinted itself upon a world in shock. A couple dozen members of the press were taken to the small hospital in the nearby town of Vallegrande, where the laundry room had hastily been conditioned to display Bolivia's trophy of unequal war. There they were permitted to observe the bodies of Che and the other two guerrillas, Willy and El Chino, captured and executed with him. Guevara's body was elevated, presented front and center, those of his two companions crumpled on the floor. Bolivian news photographer Freddy Alborta defied orders not to climb up onto the table that held the legendary guerrilla, and took a series of photographs that would become important icons, not only in keeping Che's memory alive but also in shaping that memory into the future.[5]

Those images immediately evoke the crucified Christ taken down from the cross. They show a man displayed on a cement slab, his head and torso slightly raised, long hair disheveled, naked from the waist up, torn pants and an artfully arranged jacket hiding his wounds. His lips are slightly parted—almost a faint smile—and his eyes open as if fixed on a future only he can see, one in which redemption for the world's disenfranchised is assured. On a stretcher placed over the slab-like trough, he seems to be floating, but in what? Surely not in the sordid ambience of that hastily set stage. In fact, Che had already begun to float in our collective consciousness. Death deepened and fixed forever the values he stood for in life. The message depicted in those photographic images transcends every vain hope of finality launched by Guevara's enemies. You can't kill transcendence.

Standing around the sad bier are the soldiers who participated in the hero's capture and execution. Some are young Indians, the very people whose lives Che hoped to change. Alborta's photograph would evoke comparisons both to Andrea Mantegna's *Dead Christ* and Rembrandt's *The Anatomy Lesson of Dr. Nicolaes Tulp.* In the latter, the doctor commands the attention of his students much as the high-ranking military officer in the photograph does of his troops. In both, underlings follow the gaze of the man in charge. There is always one set of eyes looking somewhere else, though. In the photographic image, while the officer points to Che's wounds, undoubtedly trying to convince the press that they all resulted from combat, one officer's gaze wanders to something going on beyond the picture plane. When searching such images for meaning, it's always a good idea to follow the wandering gaze.

Over the next years and decades many artists would produce new paintings alluding to that dramatic scene at Vallegrande. Stories of the historic day proliferated, grew, were authenticated, or simply became parts of a legend in flux. Villagers are said to have cut clumps of bloody hair to keep as relics or talismans. Candles were lit in many village homes. The people who were unable to rally around Che and his guerrilla force in life felt his power in death. Almost half a century later, impoverished residents of the area still refer to the pale Argentinean as a saint and pray to him for miracles in their hard lives.

Returning from myth to the real history of what led up to the foregoing tragedy, one must ask why a distinctively white Argentinean chose an eminently indigenous region of Bolivia as the place in which to initiate the twentieth-century continental liberation of Latin America. Porteños—the Europeanized, quick-witted, and ironic natives of Uruguay and Argentina's La Plata River basin—are viewed with distrust by the Indians of the Andes. A long-nurtured and well-founded response to racism undoubtedly played a role in the local peasants' inability to trust or support the foreigners. Che might have been more at home in northern Argentina, an area topographically similar to parts of Bolivia and with the dense vegetation so conducive to unconventional warfare.

His eventual goal included the liberation of his own country, so he would also have been geographically closer to that goal. Perhaps the failure of an earlier guerrilla attempt at Salta made him reluctant to try there again so soon.[6]

John Berger, Jean Franco, Mariano Mesman, Leandro Katz, and many others have written about the historic moment of Che's death and its cultural as well as political significance. In addition to Alborta's famous photograph, other iconic images, such as the Korda portrait and René Burri's photo of the revolutionary with his head thrown back behind a long cigar, have been reproduced by the millions—in books and magazines, on clothing and posters and coffee mugs. Thousands of poets all over the world have captured the man in verse or used his life as a point of departure for broader-ranging poems. Musical compositions, theater pieces, dance numbers, and films continue their parade of tribute or offense. For the superstitious, for progressives, for detractors, and for those disappearing few who knew the man, Che lives. Myth, religiosity, song, poetry, and art all see to that.

Here, then, is my contribution to that literature.

Che and Bee Gees, city
bus, Managua, Nicaragua, 1979.
Photo by Margaret Randall.

chapter two
in cuba, where our lives came
together in the everyday

During the volatile 1960s, I had migrated south from New York to settle in Mexico. There I married a Mexican poet, Sergio Mondragón, and we founded and coedited what would become one of the most important bilingual literary journals of the decade. *El Corno Emplumado/The Plumed Horn* published poetry, essays, narratives, letters, and drawings by cutting-edge artists crying out against the conformity and narrow academism of the times. The journal put us in touch with many of the era's most creative talents. I was still finding my way out from under the stifling McCarthyism that had swept my country of origin in the previous decade. This new creative community, with such different concerns and parameters, broadened my horizons enormously. In our issue 26, which appeared in April 1968, we reprinted John Berger's masterful essay "Che Guevara Dead."

But long before that—and much to the gratitude of US readers, for whom there was a pretty complete blackout of what was happening in Cuba—*El Corno* provided access to that country's generation of revolutionary poets. We published large selections of Cuban poetry and art in our issues 7 (July 1963) and 23 (July 1967).

And in other issues as well, letters from Cuban writers gave a sense of their lives. They were not the oppressed lives depicted in the US media, but those of exuberant and energetic men and women expressing a sense of themselves as free human beings with a world of possibility opening out before them. Artists, like everyone else, were exploring what the young revolution meant.

Despite increasing hardship, the government gave monthly stipends to a number of artists and writers so they could dedicate themselves full-time to their creative work. What did the revolution owe these artists and writers, and what did they owe the new society? Would creative people be free to follow their own voices, or would they have to contend with censorship, or both? This was one of the debates taking place at the time. Although the answers to these questions have varied over the years, in general the Cuban revolution has defended artistic freedom and produced extraordinarily significant and varied art.[1]

Within months of the guerrilla leader's death, I traveled to Cuba. It was January 1968. This was my second trip to the island. My first had been almost exactly a year earlier, when I'd joined a couple dozen Latin American poets in honoring the hundredth anniversary of Nicaraguan modernist poet Rubén Darío. This time the invitation was to a much larger gathering: the Cultural Congress of Havana. Artists, writers, performers, philosophers, psychiatrists, theoreticians, Viet Cong guerrillas, liberation theology priests, indigenous leaders, and others came together to discuss the pressing problems of a bipolar world in chaos. Images of Che were everywhere in the Cuban capital. People spoke of him in hushed voices or loudly, with pride. The sense of collective loss was palpable.

Celia Guevara, Che's younger sister, was also at that event. We became friends, took long walks together along the city's wave-swept *malecón*, the low wall that separates street from sea. Celia had a quiet sorrow about her, mixed with that sharp *rioplatense* irony so characteristic of those who live along the Rio de la Plata. One afternoon a group of us were in the Havana Libre's lobby, perhaps talking about one of the issues being debated at the congress. Celia appeared from the direction of the restroom with a wad of newsprint squares in one hand—toilet paper was at a premium back then, even in the luxury hotels: "I just can't get used to wiping my butt with my brother's face," she said, indicating the photo cut from *Bohemia* magazine, her expression a mix of humor, horror, and grief.

I never knew Che, who had disappeared from Cuba before those early visits and long before my family and I would move to the island in 1969. After our move, I developed friendships with several of his siblings and their spouses, knew his children, nephews, and nieces—some of whom went to school with my children—and made the casual acquaintance of his father, Don Ernesto Guevara Lynch. The elder Guevara resided in Cuba with his second wife and remained there until his death. Later Che's first wife, the Peruvian Hilda Gadea, became a good friend. And I got to know Alberto Granado, the man who accompanied Guevara on his famous 1952 motorcycle journey through Latin America. But all these personal relationships, slight or profound, fade in an ambience rapidly overcome by the calculated myth that makes people from Iceland to Africa feel they know the hero intimately—in most cases without knowing him at all. In Cuba, an uneven effort went into de-mystifying this myth, but popular fervor and guidelines not always up to the task have magnified it a thousandfold.

What I am interested in exploring here is that intimacy that has stayed with me all these years. Che fascinates me. And not even just the man, or the stories we have woven about him, but the sense that he personifies an era: my era. For my generation in particular, as well as several subsequent generations, there is no single name that more profoundly exemplifies our identity, our dreams, the truths we hold to be self-evident, and the cause for which we struggle. And beyond those generations familiar with the man and his history, youth everywhere continue to find in his image values to which they can relate.

Even while we who looked to Che as a leader in our effort to change society failed at so many pivotal moments in that effort, his figure remains symbolic of our deepest desires and best intentions. Later I will explore what the Che symbol may mean for social activists today, the ways in which it remains viable and the ways in which it may in fact get in the way of creating new and more relevant models of struggle and change.

Che, like many exceptional men and women, was filled with contradictions. We all harbor contradictions, of course. Perhaps the more powerful the figure, the greater or more complex his or her internal conflicts. Social restrictions of time and place may weigh heavily on such people, and their reactions to mediocrity and hypocrisy can be dramatic. With larger-than-life political, artistic, entertainment, sports, or religious figures, we may overlook or explain away such human turmoil. We expect the exceptional among us to confront injustice head-on. Che did so as a matter of course. Among his other obvious contradictions, or the ones that proved most costly, were his quick temper, his impetuousness, and a tendency to place too much trust in the presumption of morality he hoped to find in others.

Che was a man who equated social change with the powerful force of love. "Déjeme decirle, a riesgo de parecer ridículo, que el revolucionario verdadero está guiado por grandes sentimientos de amor" (Let me say at the risk of sounding ridiculous, that the true revolutionary is guided by great feelings of love).[2] This without doubt is his most frequently quoted phrase. Yet he also called for fiery conflagrations and is often perceived as having indulged in violence for its own sake.

His writings and the hundreds of thousands of pages written about him abound in examples of the man's touching observations and gestures—with an old woman dying of asthma,[3] with a child, with a comrade, with a puppy who wandered into his guerrilla camp.

Another compelling characteristic was his internationalism, his purposeful crossing of borders and his claim that wherever hunger and want existed, he felt called upon to intervene. The Argentinean from aristocratic upper-class society eagerly gave himself to the cause of poor Guatemalans, Cubans, Congolese, and Bolivians. Sometimes his transnational involvement was problematic. Sometimes it went against the basic rules of guerrilla warfare. But his refusal to limit himself to an accident of birth is what inspires me. I hate nationalism. I believe its extreme manifestations to be at the root of so many modern geopolitical biases and deceptions, so much twisted patriotism. I am thrilled by the person able to breach fabricated frontiers and follow his or her heart in an effort to learn, teach, share, and alleviate suffering.

On the other hand, and perhaps this is clearer in retrospect, it is obvious that Che's own idealism and excessive romanticism played decisive roles in his failed campaigns in Congo and Bolivia. In Cuba, he had been an internationalist fighting alongside and under the leadership of Cubans who knew their country well. At the beginning of the revolutionary war, some viewed the pale well-educated Argentinean doctor with skepticism. He spoke differently from the locals. His humor and bluntness were unexpected and unfamiliar, sometimes even offensive. He was already espousing communist ideas, mistrusted by the peasants of the Sierra. But soon his commitment, valor, and extreme sense of justice won over everyone who knew him.

In his subsequent campaigns he was the one who made the decisions, and they were not always sound ones. I have already alluded to his failure to take into account the racial and cultural contradictions inherent in his presence in Africa and in the Andean region he chose for his final theater of operations in Latin America. An insatiable need to carry the revolution to other lands clouded his vision. He was not conscious enough of local pride or of people's need or right to lead their own struggles. In many instances he put too much stock in ambiguous promises, vulnerable liaisons, faulty communication systems, and out-of-date equipment. He was obstinate in the face of Cuban and other intelligence that pointed to the desirability of waiting for more favorable circumstances or the need to create better conditions. He could be stubborn to the point of fatalism.

It isn't surprising that Che's dual identities live on in his myth, and not always in the most positive sense. During the years I lived in Cuba, every schoolchild in the country dressed in his or her maroon pants or jumper, white shirt, and red neckerchief denoting Pionero membership (the Pioneers were the youngest contingent of Communist Youth). They lined up on the playground each morning and recited in unison: "Pioneros por el comunismo, ¡seremos como el Che!" (Pioneers for communism, we will be like Che!) It was a slogan meant to instill an early reverence for justice and the will to sacrifice in the collective effort to build a more equitable society. Children shouted it automatically, much as Catholics recite the rosary or Muslims finish many sentences with "Inshala" (God willing). I often wondered if the vow might not have inhibited some of those children, who secretly feared they didn't have it in them to be like Che.

Guevara was known for the severity of his moral code and for the high demands he placed on himself and others. We know that almost from birth he suffered from an extreme case of asthma. Throughout his life he often came close to death, not only by pitting himself against the status quo in almost every situation and facing the dramatic dangers of guerrilla warfare, but also by those frequent attacks that left him gasping for the shallowest breath, his heart racing wildly. If Che could do what he did with such a physical handicap, who were we to complain or hold back? But to truly be like him? It seemed an impossible goal.

The hero's principled stance with regard to everyday situations and decisions had a profound effect on me. I too suffered from asthma; extreme attacks always brought to mind what life must have been like for Che without medication on the battlegrounds where he fought. During our years in Cuba, when the sparse ration book made grocery shopping a challenge, my determination to make do like my neighbors also drew on his example. Stories of his refusal to accept special food rations or other luxuries were legion. Perhaps in unconscious homage to him, I too refused the special ration book offered to foreigners. Our history doesn't have many examples of leaders as consistent with their stated principles. I can count them on one hand with fingers to spare. Ho Chi Minh, even when he was president of a liberated and reunified Vietnam, lived in a modest two-room house. Nelson Mandela exudes modesty. Che Guevara also rejected special privileges. These are the only three such people who come to mind.

What, however, does the aforementioned daily playground ritual teach us about leadership in general? Does it give us a useful model for promoting social change? Are there lessons to be learned about how revolutions succeed or stumble? The classic male archetype may have run its course in terms of usefulness. Feminism— and also a number of other contributions to late twentieth- and early twenty-first-century thought—suggests value in more horizontal models.

Our first few years in Cuba I applauded that slogan repeated every day by schoolchildren all over the island. It seemed in accord with the culture of the vibrant billboards proclaiming Always Forward, Never Back; If You Know, Teach, If You Don't Know, Study; Wash Your Hands; or Commander in Chief, We Await Your Orders. Slowly, though—perhaps too slowly—I came to recognize the danger in holding up a model that pristine or impossible to emulate. The daily exhortation to be like Che didn't seem to function simply as encouragement for children and adults alike to do their best. It raised the bar to unattainable heights.

I remember one of my son's friends, a very humble young man from the interior of the country, who was an example of communist youth. Before leading an assembly at which he had been charged with addressing the issue of student cheating, he realized he had a problem on his hands. He himself had cheated and didn't feel he had the moral authority to lead the assembly. He decided to confess his shortcoming. For this, he was drummed out of the Federation of University Students. Rather than take into account the value of his confession and his many other attributes, the Federation members made this fault the single focus. The punishment was implacable, devastating. I can't forget the day he came to me in tears, throwing himself into my arms, fragments of his story emerging between sobs. It is to this young man's credit that he was able to survive the shame and humiliation, stay in school, and remake his life. But I was witness to standards and to a punishment I felt were exaggerated and counterproductive.

Che's image embodied those standards.

chapter three
multiple prisms

I am a feminist, and as such I am more likely to seek inspiration in the lives of the many extraordinary women still obscured by patriarchy's refusal to give them their due than in those of men who are rendered larger than life in what remains a grossly unequal panorama. And when I look at male figures, I contemplate them through a gender lens. I consider how they live the values they profess, how they interact with women and children, what flashes of bravado or control may get in the way of their human interactions. I look for authenticity and turn away from the condescension that so often throttles communication even when they think we don't notice—or we pretend we don't. The habits are old and entrenched. The sense of entitlement rears its head when we least expect it to. In short, I am interested in how everyone—women as well as men—wields or shares power. When considering a male personality, one often has to dig beneath the surface, situating it in its historic moment but not excusing its patriarchal excesses.

In this context, Che might seem an odd attraction, yet he continues to spark my interest. I have read and reread several times everything of his that has been published. I have pored over his journals from Cuba's revolutionary war, the macabre campaign in

Interior of home, Havana, Cuba, 1970s,
images of Che and José Martí on wall.
Photo by Grandal.

Congo, and the equally doomed experience in Bolivia. I have tried to read between the lines, drawing additional insights from a man who wrote sparsely and paid more attention to the bare statistics of a skirmish with the enemy than to the emotions he worked so hard to control.[1]

I have also read most of the many biographies, written by apologists and detractors, authorized (censored?) or not by the revolution some say abandoned Guevara to his fate while claiming him for its own. And I have read a number of the books by those who fought beside him, some of them praise songs, others revelations of righteous anger in the face of a string of errors that would confound the most basic rudiments of guerrilla warfare. I have sat through films, most of which have disappointed me to varying degrees, with their vacuous biases, poor historical research, romantic idealization, and one-dimensional representation. I have pondered all these sources, keeping in mind the period, places, and cultures in which Che operated. At the same time, I naturally apply a feminist analysis of power to the choices he made and the ways in which he implemented them.

Among the major biographies, the one that seems to me the most serious—certainly the one I like best—is Pacho O'Donnell's *Che: La vida por un mundo mejor.*[2] O'Donnell, also Argentinean, comes from the same social milieu as the Guevara family and understands the man's personal and social origins. He is a psychiatrist as well as a writer and, without overemphasizing the psychological, allows us glimpses of the variety of influences that came together in Che's unique character. I'll refer to this book again later, when talking about the man's origins and youth.

Hundreds of books have been written about Che, in dozens of languages, by those who knew him or would have us believe they did. One I have gone back to several times is *Memorias de un soldado cubano: Vida y muerte de la revolución* by Dariel Alarcón Ramírez (Benigno).[3] It is not a book I take entirely at face value, but it is worth a careful read because it was written by one of the men who accompanied Che through all three of his guerrilla campaigns and one of the very few who escaped with his life after the tragedy in Bolivia. Benigno definitely has a point of view to defend, but his book seems mostly quite transparent, and ultimately heart-wrenching.

Benigno was an illiterate young peasant, isolated in a remote area of the Sierra Maestra Mountains, who joined Fidel Castro's rebels early in the revolutionary war. Che took him under his wing. The older man taught his disciple to read and write and continued to encourage him to seek an education. When the war was over, Benigno remained with Che as his assistant, bodyguard, and comrade-in-arms. He accompanied his mentor to Congo and finally to Bolivia. After the CIA's assassination of the guerrilla leader, Benigno was one of only five wounded and emaciated survivors who—breaking through the ambush that had cost Che his life, walking more than eight hundred miles, and contending with obstacles that would have stopped most—made their way halfway around the world and back to Cuba.

In Cuba Benigno and his comrades were received as heroes. They embodied the superhuman effort and mythical proportions of Latin American liberation that Cuba—at least publicly—defended without reserve. For the next couple of decades they told their extraordinary story in schools, workplaces, and at neighborhood gatherings. They were honored guests at great public rallies. And they continued to work for the revolution. Benigno, studying at night, eventually struggled through college and got his degree.

He also made several dangerous clandestine trips abroad, bringing aid to other revolutionary movements. And he headed a secret training camp in the western part of the island, from which Dominicans, Nicaraguans, Guatemalans, Chileans, Uruguayans, Argentineans, and even Mexicans[4] departed to try their luck in a number of rebel campaigns. Working with these other Latin American revolutionaries gave him insight into the problems inherent in their struggles and the degree of effective support they were receiving from Cuba.

Benigno began losing faith in the revolution he had defended with his life in so many uneven battles. More accurately, he lost faith in Fidel Castro. Although he resisted idealizing Che, the man continued to be his hero. But he came to feel that in Bolivia, at least, Fidel had abandoned him and his men. For years he'd equated the Cuban president with the revolutionary values that had given his own life such meaning. As someone who always considered himself inadequately educated, it was also easy for him to imagine that others knew more than he, or understood the complexity of a particular situation in a way he couldn't grasp. This may have been what delayed his eventual decision. Two things gnawed at him, though, and finally led him to flee Cuba, break with the revolution, and disavow so many years of unwavering faith.

One was the Bolivian campaign itself. Without exhausting all the details and endless discussions about whether or not Che and his band of revolutionaries staged their effort realistically, I will mention only a few problems about which most scholars who know the history agree. These are important not only in evaluating the decisions Che made about his own life but also in light of the fact that he took so many others with him.

One: the location of the Bolivian guerrilla. By 1967, Bolivia's population had achieved a high level of political consciousness; the mines in particular were hotbeds of revolutionary activity. But the part of the country Che chose for his campaign was sparsely populated by indigenous farmers. Many of them spoke Quechua or Guaraní, languages Che and his troop didn't know. It was the wrong place to develop a guerrilla force that, in line with the *foco* theory popular at the time, would be capable of rousing the peasantry and becoming the nucleus of a successful revolutionary movement.[5]

Members of Cuban intelligence, the French activist scholar Régis Debray,[6] and others had suggested alternative parts of the country as better suited and more appropriately populated to support an insurgency. Hundreds of pages have been written about why these places were ruled out. Without access to information that may never be revealed, I don't feel qualified to do more than make an educated guess. But there is no doubt in my mind that the area eventually decided upon was a poor choice.

There is also the question of being invited to lend aid to a guerrilla war already under way—Laurent Kabila had asked Cuba to send forces to Congo—or simply showing up where they were not invited, which was the case in Bolivia. The Bolivian Communist Party (BCP) went back and forth around supporting armed struggle, and even when it did seem amenable to that type of warfare, it wanted to retain military leadership, a demand Che would not consider. Ultimately the BCP abandoned, and in important ways even sabotaged, the guerrilla movement.

Two: the conditions for guerrilla warfare. Bolivia had established an agricultural reform law as a result of its 1952 revolution, and peasants owned the land they worked.[7] In this respect, Che couldn't argue that he and his comrades were fighting so poor farmers might own their parcels. On the contrary, the Bolivian army was able to make the locals believe the guerrillas intended to rob them of land to which they already held title. In any case, the peasants in the area where Che and his men operated were few and far between. Despite the guerrillas' attempts to engage them, they remained indifferent at best and often suspicious or frankly hostile. Various sources, including Che's own campaign diary, coincide in pointing out that during the entire eleven months of the guerrillas' presence only one farmer provided half-hearted assistance. Many denounced those they saw as foreign invaders.

Three: Cuba's support. Although Che and his group departed Cuba after careful preparation, with military training, arms, money, and a promise of logistical aid, they soon found themselves in an extremely inhospitable area and cut off from the contacts that would have enabled them to wage successful war. According to several historians, as well as Fidel himself, the guerrilla leader thought he had a commitment from the Bolivian Communist Party that it would provide the necessary infrastructure in the cities as well as additional troops. It quickly became apparent that this wasn't so.

Mario Monje, then secretary general of the BCP, visited both Cuba and the Soviet Union while Che and his men were in Bolivia. There are conflicting reports regarding the secret conversations that took place on those visits, and with the passage of time key figures have died, memories have faded, and what really happened has been only partially clarified. There are as many contradictions as "facts." It is likely that Monje informed Fidel that he wouldn't tolerate an outsider leading the struggle in his country, or that Fidel understood this between the lines.

There is plenty of evidence that the Soviets pressured the BCP leader to withhold support. Fidel himself was under a great deal of pressure from the Soviets himself, yet nevertheless he tried to get Monje to make good on his promise. Che didn't learn how alone he and his comrades were until they were on site and he and Monje had their famous meeting. From his diary entry alluding to that conversation, it is clear he knew he could no longer count on the BCP apparatus.[8] But by then his pride and determination wouldn't allow him to quit.

Soon the guerrillas' faulty radio no longer worked. There has been much conjecture as to why the guerrillas didn't have better electronic equipment, which was certainly available at the time. Then a contact, the only real liaison with Havana, was ordered to leave Bolivia for reasons that have never been satisfactorily explained. The guerrillas' isolation was complete.

Several historians have concluded that Fidel had grown ambivalent about actively supporting a guerrilla effort in Latin America. Some claim he left Che to his own devices. Cuba was deeply dependent on the Soviet Union by then, and the Soviets didn't want another revolution in the region happening outside their control. I don't buy either of these arguments. I think there is considerable evidence that Fidel did what he could to aid Che, although it wasn't enough. Before Che's final departure from Cuba, the Cuban leader begged him to delay his plans, and even argued for alternative times and places that might have proven more successful.

Despite the necessary dance he was forced to carry on with the Soviets, Fidel supported liberation struggles throughout the 1960s and 1970s and into the early 1980s. When these were authentic movements, with their own solid histories and experience, some successes occurred even under extraordinarily difficult conditions. Some of these successes were short-lived, some were able to consolidate themselves, and a few even produced revolutionary governments. Other forces may then have come into play, but there is no doubt that Cuba's successful revolution and Che's heroic effort to extend it influenced many liberation movements throughout the world.

I'm thinking particularly of the Chilean Movimiento de Izquierda Revolucionaria, or Movement of the Revolutionary Left (MIR) and even that country's Popular Unity government; the early authentic Sandinista movement in Nicaragua (FSLN); Uruguay's Tupamaros; the People's Revolutionary Party (ERP) in Argentina; the Guatemalan National Revolutionary Unity (UNRG); and the Farabundo Martí National Liberation Front (FMLN) in El Salvador. Even in the United States itself, several organizations on the radical Left took up Che's cause. The Weather Underground manifesto, printed in the pamphlet *Prairie Fire* and showing up simultaneously on doorsteps around the country, began with a section titled "Under the Banner of Che."[9]

It was when Cuba itself tried to fabricate rebel organizations that things got complicated. In such cases the guerrilla groups were nothing but agents of the Cuban revolution, without real roots in their home countries. Of course there were also a number of instances in which competing and fragmented factions within a legitimate revolutionary organization vied for Cuban support. In these cases Cuba tried to bring the factions together, or favored those it believed were most solid.

Four: other revolutionary movements. These contradictions showed themselves to varying degrees in the divisions and defeats experienced by almost all the rebels from different countries who trained in Cuba during those years. As I've pointed out, there were important differences between the homegrown movements and those created and launched by the Cubans. But there are also troubling examples of legitimate revolutionaries who came to the island to train and were kept too long against their will, returning home to fight in the worst possible conditions with little or no chance of success.

Benigno references these experiences in his book and, erroneously I believe, extrapolates from them to describe a general policy. The evidence seems to me to weigh in on the other side. It is difficult, without exhaustive research into every case, to know to what degree each of these situations was due to internal problems within the organization in question, and in how many instances they reflected contradictions in Cuba at the time. Having conversed with dozens of guerrilla fighters over the years, having even interviewed a number of them at length, I cannot accept Benigno's claim that Cuba intentionally let these movements founder.

Che Guevara and Fidel Castro,
Havana, 1962. Photo by Oswaldo Salas.

chapter four
conflicting versions

Benigno bases his conclusions on the fact that, when heading up the guerrilla training camp in Pinar del Río, he often tried to speak with Fidel and/or Manuel Piñeiro[1] about one group or another, but they invariably put him off, delaying or canceling meetings he felt were urgently needed in order for these groups to be able to move ahead with their plans. And so this man whose relationship with Che had saved him from poverty and hopelessness, this man who stood alongside him in war and peace and fought beside him in the most remote parts of the world, this man who survived his brutal murder and then his own extraordinary odyssey of escape, began to feel used. He began to doubt the story line. Although I do not entirely agree with them, I believe Benigno's conclusions are worth repeating here because they are those not of some gratuitous naysayer or devil's advocate, but of someone willing to risk his life beside the man in whom he believed, and did so repeatedly.

He knew enough not to be taken in by that other, fabricated narrative put forth by those whose goal it was to discredit Castro and the Cuban revolution. He knew, for example, that Fidel had not murdered Che—a preposterous tale repeated among exiles and others in the political opposition. But he also came to believe that things had not been exactly as Cuba claimed they were. He himself had experienced many of the discrepancies. He retained his love and respect for Che, but began to suspect that Fidel was no longer the man he had admired in the Sierra Maestra. Benigno's position and eventual defection have been much maligned by supporters of the Cuban revolution for whom criticism is unacceptable. These supporters tolerate nothing less than what they see as total loyalty. In my mind, loyalty is worth more when it is able to express valid questions.

Clearly Fidel was in a difficult situation with regard to Cuba's support of the revolutionary movements in the Americas, including the one headed by his old comrade-in-arms. The Soviets were insistent. It was easier for Cuba to play a role in Africa, where the Soviet Union was not then juggling its precarious relationship with the United States and where it also lent important assistance. But I think history shows that in Latin America as well, Cuba managed to stay true to its ideals.

There is also evidence that Fidel did try to dissuade his old friend from leaving the island until the infrastructure in Bolivia could be more fully developed. Several letters exist in which he proposed waiting or exploring alternative options. And there are moving references to a conversation between the two men at the training camp in Pinar del Río province on the eve of Che's final departure. Witnesses to this conversation, who couldn't overhear their words but observed their gestures, speak of a powerful embrace followed by a long period of silence, after which Fidel got up and walked away. The image that remains exudes resignation as well as abiding friendship.

Che was restless, impatient. The debacle in Congo had taken its toll.[2] He had contributed his intelligence and energies to the transformations in Cuba and felt there was little left for him to do there. And he longed to embark on the liberation of Latin America, the dream he had nurtured for so long.

As for Benigno—and here again this goes to his evaluation of Fidel and the Cuban revolution as a whole, not his feelings about Che—the other element that began to grate on him was the corruption he saw among government and party officials: stolen resources, luxurious mansions, and other privileges in a country still besieged by hardship and scarcity. Benigno took part in the Cuban campaign in Angola and writes indignantly about Cuban planes returning to the island filled with ivory, gemstones, domestic appliances, and other exotic items. He claims that these were looted from the Angolan people and that most of them found their way into the homes of Cuban leadership, or to the dollar stores where those leaders and foreign workers did their shopping. It is important to note that Benigno does not accuse Fidel of personally benefiting from this sort of looting or corruption. He mentions other officials, never the maximum leader. But in Cuba there has long been the sense—true or not—that Fidel knows everything that goes on. If it happens, the popular perception is that he either allows it to happen and chooses to look the other way or is a participant.

Benigno also writes poignantly about the great sacrifice made by the thousands of Cubans who fought in Africa—not just Angola but other countries as well—and the terrible numbers of Cuban dead. He says he began to realize that in a system that proclaimed equality, a few lived in stolen luxury while the vast majority sacrificed themselves at home or on internationalist missions.

I know about Cuban corruption. I saw it during the eleven years my family and I lived in that country and have seen it on visits since. It is distressing, often criminal. But I have tried to place it within the context of a people who have sacrificed so much and gone without for so long. The revolution's tremendous advances in legal equality, equitable distribution of resources, health care, education, sustainable agriculture, housing, science, sports, the arts, and those unquantifiable resources called dignity and solidarity stand as impressive achievements. To me, the overall efforts to create a more just society vastly outweigh these serious but sporadic blemishes.

Certainly there is an important difference between a government official who steals in order to adorn his large home with African leopard skins or ivory, and an ordinary working man or woman who frequents the black market or hustles to provide additional food for his or her family. The same distinction can be made here in the United States between the big bankers who have made millions squandering the savings of ordinary citizens, on the one hand, and a homeless family that moves into an empty house, on the other. I am not convinced that corruption in Cuba is anywhere near the level that exists in the United States or in many other countries. On the other hand, there is no excuse for this sort of behavior on the part of those who claim to be fighting for justice.

It may seem that I am straying from my ruminations about Che. But the foregoing is important in terms of evaluating not only Benigno's desertion of the Cuban revolution (and thus his story's relevance to Che's conduct and goals), but also the situation on various guerrilla fronts and the man who was Ernesto Guevara. Che's marked rejection of luxury of any kind and the example he set by not allowing himself or his family to benefit from such privilege highlight his concern with corruption and how it might corrode social change in Cuba.

Che knew it would be hard to change generations of capitalist and consumerist values. He was familiar with capitalist economics and also an assiduous student of the theories being implemented in the Soviet Union, China, and other socialist countries. He wrote and spoke at length about the problems he saw in the Soviet model. Since China, although so much larger than Cuba, was also an eminently agricultural economy, it seemed to him to hold the more applicable solutions. He also found Vietnamese solutions interesting. But Che was always studying, and he designed his own recipe for bringing Cuba out of dependent capitalism and pointing it toward a more diversified and egalitarian economy. Had he lived, there is no doubt in my mind he would have been insatiable in examining yet other models and exploring other solutions.

The stories of his morality are legion. When he discovered that his family was receiving extra food rations without his consent—a situation that angered and shamed him—he put an immediate end to it. Once when he entertained a distinguished guest for dinner in his office, and the ministry's chef brought him the same meal, he angrily refused it, preferring his usual simpler fare. When he was minister of industry and president of the national bank, he labored hours no human could be expected to keep on a regular basis. When those who worked with him said they could no longer continue at his pace, he agreed to shorten their workday from seven in the morning to one a.m. the following! His was a consistent example of doing more, without accepting the perks others took for granted. He believed revolutionaries had to set a tone of sacrifice and austerity and was invariably the first in that endeavor.

Cuban flag and Che poster,
exterior wall, Havana, Cuba, 1990s.
Photo by Margaret Randall.

chapter five

"socialism and man in cuba"

I want to move from what others have written about Che to "El socialismo y el hombre en Cuba" ("Socialism and Man in Cuba"), the 1965 letter he penned to Carlos Quijano, editor of the influential Left Uruguayan weekly, *Marcha*.[1] Evaluating Che's thought today, one might go to a number of sources. Guevara made important international speeches at the Special Meeting of the Inter-American Economic and Social Council of the Organization of American States in Punta del Este, Uruguay, in 1961, and before the UN General Assembly in 1964. Both provide insights into imperialism's domination of developing nations, Cuba's place in the world, and the longing for change on the part of peoples everywhere. At Punta del Este, Comandante Guevara accurately represented his adopted country's positions. At the UN, he strayed somewhat from official policy, laying himself open to severe criticism from Fidel on his return to Cuba.

Other rich resources are Che's three campaign diaries (from the Cuban war, his time in Congo, and his final guerrilla effort in Bolivia). These, augmented by all that he wrote on the art of guerrilla warfare itself, give us a detailed understanding of his ideas on strategy and tactics in irregular conflict. Additionally, there are dozens of important essays, speeches, and interviews done with him by others, on topics ranging from education to economics and work. He wasn't academically trained in any of these disciplines, but he was insatiably curious, accumulated a great deal of experience, read widely, and his power of analysis was acute.

The Che of popular culture is much more a man of action than ideas. With the passage of time, even students of his life tend to focus more on his guerrilla struggles than on his thought. But Che was an original thinker, and one who contributed a great deal to our understanding of the problems inherent in trying to change society so that exploitation is a thing of the past and human beings may reach their full potential. His power comes primarily from the risks he took in using, but not feeling bound by, traditional theory. It is evident in his brilliant fusion of experience and analysis.

I want to focus on "Socialism and Man in Cuba" precisely because it was written in 1965. Che's formative years were behind him. He had seen a great deal of the world, both as an anonymous youth exploring the capitals and back ways of his beloved continent and as the representative of a revolution in power. He had chalked up extraordinary experiences on the battlefield and in the construction of a new society. His final scenario—the guerrilla front in Bolivia—was still ahead. In this letter, Che's observations come from a pivotal moment in his life, one in which he may have achieved his greatest balance. Although penned aboard an airplane returning from Africa, they encompass a great deal of his accumulated wisdom. This letter seems to me to be his greatest written legacy. Certainly for my generation it was an iconic text.

Che begins by talking about an issue he knew troubled many when they contemplated revolutionary change: the fear that in socialism the individual would be swallowed up by the state. He references Cuba's recent history, noting that during the guerrilla stage the population was composed of vanguard leaders, on the one hand, and masses of ordinary people, on the other. The latter were largely uninformed and complacent, but the former were able to rally them through outreach and example. This is very much in line with the ideas that nurture the *foco* theory and the premises of guerrilla warfare in general.

Che goes on to trace Cuba's rebel war and the months following its victory, when the challenge was to establish a new type of government, one guided by ideals of justice and responsive to human need. He emphasizes the importance of a brilliant, transparent, and charismatic figure at the helm, capable of organizing such a total political, economic, and social overhaul. In Cuba that leader was Fidel Castro.

But almost immediately, Che surprises us by stating that between such a leader and the masses, the masses are the more important protagonist. People who simply follow a leader can't change society; only empowered people can. Che writes that, seen superficially, it might appear that those who speak of the subordination of the individual to the state are correct. But he goes on to show that the state will inevitably commit errors and that each of these errors decreases popular enthusiasm and support. In this way, the masses act as a necessary check on leadership gone awry.

Che speaks about the laws of capitalism, always invisible to those it manipulates. He writes that in that inhuman system the prize remains distant, and one can only reach it on the shoulders of others' failures. For the new society in formation, he says, the past is a formidable adversary:

This past makes itself felt not only in human consciousness, where the residue of an education systematically oriented toward isolating the individual still weighs heavily, but also through the very character of this transitional period in which commodity relations persist. Commodity is the driving force of capitalism. So long as it exists, its effects will make themselves felt in the organization of production and thus in human consciousness.

Marx outlined the transitional period that follows the explosive transformation of the capitalist system when it is destroyed by its own contradictions. In historical reality, however, we have seen that those countries that were the weakest limbs on imperialism's tree were torn off first. Lenin predicted this phenomenon.

In these countries, capitalism had developed to the point where people felt its effects in one way or another. But it wasn't capitalism's internal contradictions alone that, having exhausted all possibilities, caused the system to come apart. The struggle for liberation from a foreign oppressor, the misery caused by external events such as wars, the consequences of which the privileged classes place on the backs of the exploited, liberation movements aimed at overthrowing neo-colonial regimes: any of these can unleash this kind of explosion. Conscious action takes it from there.[2]

Che returns to the role of the individual in social change:

I would like to explain the role personality plays, individual men and women who lead the masses that make history. This is only our experience, not a prescription for others. It is not a matter of how many pounds of meat one has to eat, or of how many times a year one can go to the beach, or how many pretty things from abroad one might be able to buy with today's wages. It's a matter of making the individual feel more complete, with much more inner wealth and much more responsibility.

Regarding dogmatism, Che is absolutely clear that avoiding it depends first and foremost on the leadership's refusal to indulge itself in privileges not available to everyone:

We may incur weaknesses. . . . In our case we have been careful that our own children possess or lack those things that the children of the ordinary citizen have or lack. Our families must understand this and make sure it's really so.

A revolution is made by individuals, but individuals must sharpen their revolutionary spirit every day.

Che also explored dogmatism in art. What he said about artistic creativity was groundbreaking for the time:

> When the revolution took power there was an exodus on the part of those who were the most comfortable. The rest, revolutionaries or not, discovered a new way forward. Artistic inquiry experienced a renewed impulse. The pathways had already been established, though, and the escapist concept hid itself behind the word "freedom." We even found this attitude among revolutionaries themselves, a reflection of their bourgeois-idealist consciousness.
>
> In countries that have gone through a similar process, attempts have been made to combat such tendencies with exaggerated dogmatism. Cultural values literally became taboo, and accurately portraying nature was thought to be the pinnacle of artistic aspiration. Later this was transformed into a mechanical copy of the social reality they wanted to showcase: the ideal society, almost without conflicts or contradictions, which they sought to create.
>
> Socialism is young and has made mistakes. We revolutionaries often lack the knowledge and intellectual audacity required to meet the challenge of developing a new man and woman whose methods are unconventional. Conventional methods suffer from the imprint of the society that gave birth to them. (Once again, the subject of the relationship between form and content is posed.) Disorientation is widespread, and the problems of material construction absorb us. There are no artists of great authority who have great revolutionary authority as well. The members of the party must . . . educate the people.
>
> What predominates, then, is simplification, something everyone can understand, something functionaries under-

stand. True artistic experimentation ends, and the problem of general culture is reduced to assimilating the socialist present and the dead (i.e., non-threatening) past. Thus socialist realism arises upon the foundations of the art of the last century. The realistic art of the 19th century, however, also has its class character, more purely capitalist perhaps than the decadent art of the 20th century that reflects the anguish of the alienated individual. In the field of culture, capitalism has given all it had to give. . . . But why try to find the only valid prescription in the frozen forms of socialist realism? We must not oppose "freedom" with socialist realism, because the former does not yet exist and will not exist until the complete development of a new society. We must not, from the pontifical throne of realism-at-all-costs, condemn all forms of art since the first half of the 19th century, for we would then fall into the Proudhonian error of getting stuck in the past, of straight-jacketing the artistic expression of those who are being born and are in the process of creating themselves.

As a poet and artist, I find this analysis to be visionary among social activists of the time. Sadly, it continues to have relevance.

Che closes with a series of concise conclusions, some of which I will transcribe:

We socialists are freer because we are more fulfilled; we are more fulfilled because we are freer.

The skeleton of our complete freedom is already formed; what's lacking is the flesh and clothing. These we will create.

Our freedom and its daily support system are paid for in blood, and swollen with sacrifice. Our sacrifice is conscious; it's the price we pay for the freedom we create.

The road is long and partially unknown; we are aware of our limitations. We will give birth to the man of the twenty-first century: ourselves.

I have gone into such detail in quoting from and speaking about this letter because I believe it contains important kernels of Guevarian thought, particularly with regard to human creativity and art. In translating these fragments, I have been careful to remain faithful to Che's language. His title, which fails to honor his inclusion of women in the text itself, is clearly an impediment for me. He, of course, would have claimed he included women. But for someone with such rich linguistic talent, it is not a convincing argument.

I can try to justify this bias by referencing the historic period. Feminism had not yet brought public attention to language's gendered implications. Still, I must admit to a deep disappointment at Che's inability to go beyond the moment in this respect. It pains me that someone whose brilliance shone in so many ways would not have noticed he was speaking to only half the human race. As with so many of our great architects, I take that which is valuable while lamenting the absence of what might have been. In "Socialism and Man in Cuba" I find a great deal that is valuable.

But I also lament the fact that at the time this letter was written so many strong women, myself included, didn't even notice our absence in such texts! We devoured them, engaging with their analyses of the world in which we lived, completely unaware that they wrote us out of history. Oh, how I would have loved sparring with Che about his failure to explicitly name women in the title of a letter this important.

Just a few years later we would enter a time of renovation in ideology and in struggle, in thought and in the language with which we expressed that thought. I remember my own early contacts with feminism and how profoundly they changed me. During my first years in Cuba I often stopped men who shouted vulgarities on the street and challenged their right to offend. My teenage daughters didn't want to go out with me, embarrassed by their mother's loud complaints. Only much later would they come to appreciate my attitude. Around the same time, discussions with a poet friend just before he went back to his country, and ultimately to his death, re-

sulted in some of his last poems being written in a female voice—
and expressing feminist values. Those poems still thrill me.[3]

Do we expect too much from our visionaries?

Yes, of course. And I think we should expect everything from
them, although we often have to settle for less.

chapter six
tender heart and rigorous moral code

Among Cuban revolutionaries, Che was famous for shunning privilege of any sort. I've already mentioned that he was exemplary of someone whose moral code would not allow special rations, much less an ostentatious home or other luxury items. He wouldn't stand for these privileges being afforded his wife or children either. This was all part of his consistency in not simply talking the talk but walking the walk—the consistency that continues to make him such a compelling figure. In their writings, his widow, Aleida March, and Che himself both mention a ring he had apparently promised to buy her on one of his trips abroad. In her memoir, March reproduces a letter from Che in which he explains that he's sorry but in light of the hardship still plaguing the country he just couldn't bring himself to spend money on such an expensive gift.

Rigorous and directed as he undoubtedly was, evidence also exists of an extraordinary tenderness laced with his unique intelligence. I could quote from many examples. In one of the interviews Fidel gave about Che after the latter's death, he spoke of how, during Cuba's revolutionary war, Guevara was tending to the wounded. One of his men was dying. There was nothing the guer-

Last known photo of
Che and his family, Havana,
Cuba, 1965. Photo courtesy
Guevara Family Archive.

rilla doctor could do to save him, so he simply leaned down and kissed him on the forehead.

One story I find particularly moving is transcribed by March in her book about their life together. It was early 1966. Che had left Congo after his discouraging defeat in that African country. Husband and wife had been able to spend a couple of weeks together in Prague before he continued toward his final campaign in Bolivia. The following is excerpted from one of the last letters he would write to her:

My love:

The moment has come to send you a farewell tasting of earth (dry leaves, something distant and discarded). I would like to have been able to do this with lines that don't reach the margins — often called poems — but I haven't been able.

There are so many intimate things for your ears alone, and words turn to prisons inhibiting my feelings. They are but the shy algorithms that try to break through my usual manner of speech. . . . I am not made for the poet's noble profession. And it's not that I don't have sweet things to say. If you only knew all that whirls around inside me. But the spiral shell holding those words is too long, too convoluted and narrow. They emerge from the journey exhausted, grumpy, all wrong. And the sweetest of all are so fragile! They have shattered along the way, becoming disperse vibrations, nothing more.

I am alone in this, so I must open myself in order to tell you what I feel. Let me use everyday language, snapshots of remembered moments.

. . . I love you as I recall our bitter morning coffee, the taste of the dimple on your knee, a bit of delicately balanced cigar ash, the incoherent grumbling with which you defend your impregnable pillow. . . .

That is how I love you, watching the children grow, like

a staircase without its history (and I suffer because I can no longer see those steps). Every day it is like a knife in my side, upbraiding the idler from his shell.

This will be the real farewell. Five years in the struggle have aged me. Now there's only one last step—the definitive one.

The siren songs and internal battles are done. The starting gate has opened on my last race. I will be moving so fast all screams will flee me. The past is finished. I am a future on its way.

Don't call me. I won't be able to hear you. I'll only be able to feel you on sunny days, beneath the renewed caress of bullets. . . .

I'll cast a spiral glance, like the final return of a dog looking for a place to lie down, and I'll touch you all with my eyes, one by one and the lot of you together.

If one day you feel the sudden violence of my presence, don't turn around, don't break the spell, just keep on making my coffee and let me experience you forever in that perennial instant.[1]

Each image in this letter is worth careful attention for what it tells us about the man, his self-image, philosophy of life, and his attitude toward his closest relationships. With time running out—and he must have sensed this in some deep way—he imagines (almost as if speaking of a lover) a "caress of bullets" and visualizes himself "moving so fast all screams will flee" from him. He defines himself as "a future on its way." In a relatively brief letter, expressions of sweet love are punctuated by others that evoke the warrior.

In this letter I find the references to a "spiral shell . . . too long, too convoluted and narrow" and "I'll cast a spiral glance, like the final return of a dog looking for a place to lie down" to be particularly interesting. Feminist poets especially have used the spiral to denote nonlinear time and emotion, concepts that belie the more masculine narrative. In the man's writing, glimpses such as these whisper to me that, had he lived, he might have surprised us with a complexity not remarked upon by many who have examined Che's life.

At mid-twentieth century, Dominicans, Haitians, Bolivians, Peruvians, Nicaraguans, Colombians, Argentineans, Chileans, Guatemalans, Mexicans, Uruguayans, and other Latin Americans dreamed of bringing justice to their homelands through the force of arms. Dozens of these men, and the smaller number of women involved, had varying degrees of contact with Che in Cuba. They lived in small groups in houses hidden from mainstream Cuban life and studied guerrilla warfare in secret training camps throughout the island. Sometimes they waited weeks or months before receiving the anticipated order to depart for the front.

Late at night, after his tremendously overburdened workday, Che might drop by the places where these rebels were housed, to talk, share ideas, and encourage them. A number of Che's biographers have been fortunate enough to interview survivors of this select group. Two themes repeat themselves in their testimonies. One describes the man's extraordinary sensibility, his talent for touching the intimate longings and trembling uncertainties of a generation's most generous and sacrificial spirits. The other is Che's unusual combination of theoretician and warrior. History has given us great thinkers and powerful actors, but rarely both qualities in a single person.

In the less intimate, more public arena, there is the famous discussion of moral as opposed to material incentives. I touched on this briefly in the previous chapter ("Socialism and Man in Cuba"). The debate has been mischaracterized by a number of Che's biographers as well as by those who have written about the Cuban revolution overall. Guevara never proposed moral incentives as exclusive payment for voluntary work, nor did he believe that material incentives had no role in revolution. Jon Lee Anderson goes into some detail about

> Che's insistence upon the application of "moral incentives" *in addition to* "material incentives." The system employed in the Soviet Union had grown out of the New Economic Policy (NEP) adopted by Lenin in 1921,[2] as a way of jump-starting the stagnant Soviet economy after the civil war. Che believed that system prevented workers from achieving a true socialist regard for their labor, a regard only moral incentives could achieve.[3]

The foregoing—in real terms and in legend—is all part of that myth that is larger than life and that presents Cuban schoolchildren with such a dilemma. Che was a profoundly principled person, and this often showed itself in a certain rigidity. His own writings are filled with examples of having ordered the execution of soldiers who made mistakes that might put the whole troop in danger or who, in a moment of extreme hunger, had stolen an extra can of condensed milk. Some of these tales are accompanied by admissions of regret, even self-criticism. Yet many who have studied Che's life link those incidents to his role, immediately following the revolutionary victory, in overseeing the hasty execution of Batista's best-known torturers—at least those who hadn't been able to get away.

But Che also instituted the practice, in Bolivia and in the Cuban war, of releasing captured prisoners after lecturing them about his movement's goals. Some of these men, clearly impressed, defected to the side of the guerrilla. Others, of course, returned to their base of operations with valuable information about where the rebel forces were located. Some analysts would argue that Che erred in both directions or that the essence of his behavior was linked neither to excessive severity nor to a capacity for forgiveness but, rather, to unwaveringly following whatever arbitrary rules he may have established at a given time. His conduct seemed to reflect an attitude complicit with the terms of war rather than a case-by-case assessment.

Che's consciousness and rejection of racial inequality is evident throughout his public declarations, as in his early speech at Las Villas University, in which he said:

> The days when education was a privilege of the white middle class have ended. The University must paint itself black, mulatto, worker, and peasant. It must paint itself black, brown and yellow. If it does not, the people will break down its doors and paint it the colors they like.

This was a reference to the fact that prior to the revolution in Cuba a university education had been accessible only to upper-class whites and that profound systemic change must deliver it for all.

This consciousness makes one wonder all the more how Che could have been so oblivious to the inappropriateness of his presence in Congo. The Cuban troops who went to the African country were all black; their leader was a pale white man from an entirely different culture.

And this is where my fascination with the man often comes to rest. I do believe he was unusually unselfish, non-self-indulgent, goal-oriented, and pure (I use that word with all intention). I also know he was narrowly directed and could be extremely single-minded. There is a certain arrogance that many great men and women possess, or a quality others read as arrogance. Is this an endemic or necessary quality in such people? I fervently hope we can find ways to celebrate nonarrogant forms of leadership. That we can draw out, in future leaders, the kind of purity Che displayed — but without that edge of superiority. That we can seek alternative forms of struggle and interaction that are less hierarchical, self-involved, and patriarchal than those twentieth-century archetypes.

Alberto Granado and Ernesto Guevara
on a raft on the Amazon River, June 1952.
Photographer unknown.

chapter seven
empowerment of the erotic

Because sex goes a long way toward creating a hero and selling the myth, there has been a great deal of talk about the women in Che's life. It is known that when he departed Argentina as a very young man on that first famous motorcycle trip, he left behind a girl from his social milieu with whom he was crazy in love. Alberto Granado, the friend and travel companion who documented that journey, wrote that Guevara tried to convince the young woman to wait for him, but she made it clear she didn't consider him acceptable husband material. She did give him fifteen dollars, though, to buy her a bikini if he made it to Miami. Despite serious bouts of hunger, without a peso to his name, he never spent those fifteen dollars. Years later, after the victory in Cuba, he sent her the bikini by way of his mother, who had visited him there.

It was during Che's travels through Latin America that he met Hilda Gadea, the woman who would become his first wife. She was a Peruvian of distinctly Andean body type and features, an economist and already an experienced activist for social change. She contributed meaningfully to his political education. It is clear that she fell deeply in love with him and that he reciprocated at least to some degree. He also used the relationship, as so many men (and women) sometimes do, to partake of female company, assuage his loneliness, and pass the time. His first loyalty was always to the revolution. Hilda became pregnant, so they married and had a daughter. But once Che joined Fidel's forces and embarked on the Granma,[1] they never lived together again.

At the end of the war, Hilda and Hildita came to reside in Cuba. For Che it was probably an arrangement that allowed him to be close to his daughter; for Hilda, an opportunity to be near the man she still loved and to work within the new revolutionary society. Although this is rarely emphasized by historians, Gadea herself had actively participated in the Cuban revolutionary movement in exile.

By this time Guevara was in a relationship with the woman who was to become his second wife, Aleida March, with whom he would have four more children. They met in the Sierra, where she was involved in revolutionary support work. They married as soon as he was able to secure the divorce from Gadea. A range of interviews, letters, and other evidence points to Aleida March as the romantic love of Che's life. Both Gadea and March have written interesting books about their years with the *guerrillero heróico*; Gadea's is the more political text, March's the more intimate.[2] March is the undeniable widow, though. As such, and as a historian, she runs the Che Guevara Study Center, which preserves the official documentation on Che's life—all his original manuscripts and ephemera—and promotes an understanding of his work.

Having studied Che from a variety of directions, I don't personally believe he was a serious womanizer. Even his marriages were absolutely subservient to his life as a revolutionary, a fact that must have been painful for his wives and children despite the fact that they shared his principles. He didn't drink, wasn't known for extramarital affairs, and was always extremely critical of fellow combatants when they visited prostitutes. He never expressed derogatory views of women forced to sell their bodies; on the contrary, when he mentioned them it was always with an understanding of the social conditions that pushed them into that exploitative occupation. For Che and for most other authentic revolutionaries of his time, the struggle always came first. Relationships with wives and children, even when loving, were a distant second.

I am not interested in the other women with whom Che may or may not have had romantic relationships. The stories are short on evidence and long on the sort of titillation that feeds the scandal-hungry imagination—at both political extremes. In Che's diary of the Cuban campaign, he mentions some of the women involved in the movement, always with great respect. Women are absent from his writing about the campaign in Congo, except when he talks about the prostitutes visited by local troops; there didn't seem to have been any females among the Congolese soldiers.

In Bolivia there was Tania, the famous young German-Argentinean woman who was part of the rearguard but who, after a visit to the guerrilla camp, was unable to make it back to the city.[3] She ended up assuming a role in the bedraggled force and died in an ambush several months before Che. Several biographers and much popular lore have made Che and Tania into a romantic couple. I find the suggestion irrelevant. Tania herself has left written evidence that she was in love with Ulysses Estrada, a high-level member of the Cuban department that oversaw its aid to foreign insurgencies. Loyola Guzmán and several other women also played notable roles in the Bolivian campaign. As they did not possess Tania's internationalist background or European-type beauty, the mythmakers have refrained from linking them romantically to Che.

Che's longtime friendship with Cuban revolutionary heroine Haydée Santamaría was in a category of its own. In a later chapter I explore it at length, first because Haydée embodied some of the same unusual characteristics Che possessed. National cultures shape individual attributes. For brief periods of time revolutionary cultures do this even more intensely. It was Haydée who once said she didn't know if Ho Chi Minh was the kind of person he was because he was Vietnamese, or if it was the other way around: that the Vietnamese people were influenced by having Ho at the center of their lives. The same might be said of certain figures who loomed larger than life in the dynamic early years of the Cuban revolution, and Che and Haydée were such figures. Another reason I devote a chapter to the two of them is that I feel a kinship between how I perceive their relationship to have been and my own haunting connection to both.

Although I find the many rumors linking Che with different women irrelevant to a consideration of the man, this is no reason to ignore Che's physical attraction. Eroticism is a far deeper concept than what romantic histories alone can convey.

I am sure that Guevara, like most of his contemporaries, saw men as superior in terms of biological conditioning, physical strength, the ability to fight, and the detachment from family ties that presumably enables them to endure long military missions. In this, he was a man of his time. On the other hand, he often relied on women as strategists, tacticians, messengers, experts in infrastructure, and trusted liaisons, taking their advice seriously and depending on their expertise. And he went further than most. In his important manual *Guerrilla Warfare*, he writes:

> Women can play an extraordinarily important role in a
> revolutionary process. It is important to emphasize this be-
> cause the colonial mentality that reigns in all our countries
> has produced real discrimination against them. Women are
> capable of carrying out the most difficult tasks, of fighting
> alongside men and, contrary to what many believe, if the
> troop has the right organization and ideological training
> they do not create sexual conflict.[4]

Since Che did not live at a time when traditional ideas about women were being publicly challenged, it is impossible to know whether he would have been open to a feminist ideology or would have understood what feminism tells us about the nature of power.

His almost exclusive concern with taking power through the force of arms leads me to believe he might not have been able to embrace the change. His enormously curious mind and deep intelligence tell me he might have. Today we more easily see that it is through the multiple and contested narratives of public discourse that reality, thought, interpretation, and opinion are constantly made, unmade, and remade.[5]

Although the figure of Che doesn't speak to me sexually, it possesses a deep and compelling eroticism. I use the term "erotic" in Audre Lorde's conception:

> The principal horror of any system which defines the good
> in terms of profit rather than in terms of human need, or
> which defines human need to exclusion of the psychic and
> emotional components of that need—the principal horror
> of such a system is that it robs our work of its erotic value,
> its erotic power and life appeal and fulfillment.[6]

The erotic here is embodied in a man who combined deep commitment with the psychic, emotional, and physical components of the struggle for justice. That struggle embraces a powerful eroticism.

If Che's ideas about gender were only slightly better than the norm for his place and time, his attitude toward sexual difference was probably similar. Writers have pointed critically to his use of the derogatory term *maricón* (faggot) to describe a male who disgusted him for some reason, who showed cowardice, or whom he wanted to offend. Without condoning the offensive term, I think it important to point out that this epithet was used freely at the time, especially in the grossly macho society in which Che operated. I am not convinced that on his lips it carried a specifically homophobic intention. I have not been able to find evidence that Che participated in the shameful repression of homosexuals that tarnished the Cuban revolution's early years. The absence of his name linked to repressive acts against those not in the sexual mainstream, at a time when he was prominent in the revolutionary leadership, tells me this was not something with which he was personally involved.

Many have emphasized brutality or an exaggerated desire for revenge, evidenced in the postwar executions. Some have accused Che of ordering those executions without a second thought. A number of historians, on the other hand, say he suffered them stoically like he suffered so much else and that he actually commuted at least half the capital sentences. Even taking into consideration the culture of the time, though, I do believe Che often erred on the side of violence when confronted with problems requiring expedient solutions. What I call violence he may have seen as necessary severity or a requirement of rigorous command. His mentality, after all, was that of a soldier.

As to the broader issue of capital punishment, I cannot help but wonder if Che would have continued to support such an impoverished policy had he lived long enough to reassess his ideas in the context of subsequent cultural change. Here, as in other areas, only personal conjecture is possible, and I take responsibility for mine. At the time in which those executions took place, the Cuban people en masse cried out for immediate and severe punishment. Guevara was a foreigner, and it is reasonable to assume that he took leadership from the Cubans on this and other issues. At the same time, there is no evidence that he had a moral aversion toward the death penalty or was interested in pacifism as a viable ideological position.

Che was someone who never stopped reading and studying. He loved debate and was capable of self-criticism or of changing his mind about something when convinced he'd been wrong. His extreme sensibility comes through in almost all his writings and speeches, and although he defended the principles for which he lived and died with a ferocity rarely seen in others, he was not above embracing new ideas.

By the above paragraphs I mean to imply that Che was both a visionary and a man of his time and social class — the Argentinean aristocracy that no longer had the wealth to live as it once had and so was forced to make up in social convention what it lacked in money. He inherited, and also acquired along the way, many distortions typical of that time and class. But he was also, and powerfully, a man of hard-won personal convictions. In the end he betrayed his class privilege as few others have.

Che with his mother,
Celia de la Serna, Havana 1959.
Photographer unknown.

chapter eight
how the man was made

In his biography, Pacho O'Donnell brings to bear a psychiatrist's assessment. Among other things, he points out that Che's parents weren't married when they conceived him, a situation that was considered shameful in the society in which they lived. The date of his birth, celebrated round the world as June 14, was actually a month earlier, on May 14. So, shame at the root, and all that which shame engenders.

Almost from birth, their first child suffered from acute asthma, necessitating the family's frequent moves to find a climate that would improve his health. Attacks severe enough to keep young Ernesto in bed for protracted periods pushed him to try to excel at particularly rough sports such as rugby. Schoolmates and other childhood friends testify to his dogged participation in the toughest of these, even as he often broke up fights and chastised kids who shot birds or were cruel to animals. From his earliest years, he demonstrated the will to succeed at activities much too physically hard for him, while disavowing brutality for brutality's sake. This childhood abhorrence of violence might seem to fly in the face of later choices. The contradiction can best be explained, I believe, when we understand that in the struggle against an enemy of such vastly superior strength, all efforts had to be considered legitimate.

From shortly after his birth and for the next eight years, Ernesto was cared for by Carmen Arias, a Galician woman who was his nanny. She remained close to the family even after she married and returned to Spain. Many years later, on trips to Uruguay or Argentina, Che made time to visit with her or her relatives.

Both of Guevara's parents were important influences, at times because of their beliefs and actions, and at times because they embodied attitudes he rejected or against which he could test his own developing ideology.

Ernesto Guevara Lynch, like many liberals independent of their country of origin, defended a series of progressive causes but was less inclined—as his oldest son so definitively would be—to incorporate those values into his everyday life. He did, however, actively support the Spanish Republic, and when Ernesto was a child he and his father attended many events in support of the rebels in that "last just war." These events seem to have been important to the son's early understanding of liberation struggles.

The older Guevara was a man who struggled to find his passion in life. He worked at a variety of jobs, generally failing at them (sometimes because he couldn't bring himself to be as bloodthirsty as his competitors). He had a series of mistresses, some of whom he introduced into the Guevara home, to his wife's humiliation and anger. Eventually the couple divorced.

As soon as the Cuban war ended, with Ernesto having been one of its principal protagonists, his parents and siblings visited the Caribbean country. On more than one occasion his father embarrassed Che by expecting special treatment—against which the son always raged. The older Guevara eventually made his home on the island, where he remarried, and he lived there until he died. After Che's death, Don Ernesto's new wife gave birth to children decades the hero's junior. Che's progenitor wrote a book called *Young Che*[1] and spent his last years publishing collections of letters and other writings by his famous firstborn. In an ironic twist, but one that occurs in a number of families, the son's life became the subject of the father's most successful career.

It would be precisely in one of these books—a laborious work of compilation—that the older Guevara would give us the deepest insight into his son's early life and formation. In *Young Che: Memories of Che Guevara by His Father*, he reproduces fragments from Ernesto's early journals, letters home and to friends, and lengthy written dialogues with several lifelong companions. These documents, taken together and in chronological order, offer us one way of following Che's journey to the political consciousness and conviction that would shape his later life.

It is through these texts—most authored by Che himself, a few written to or about him and interspersed with the father's retrospective analysis—that we understand the man's evolution and the absolute harmony between his intellectual convictions and his action. His brilliance shines. He had obtained his medical degree in a remarkably short time, largely through reading, hands-on practice, and sitting for exams. Curiosity was a constant, and on several journeys through the countries of America (the famed motorcycle trip was only one of these), he got beneath the surface of each place visited by traveling with and working among its poorest citizens, studying voraciously, and analyzing all the political forces at play.

Ernesto's parents feared for their son's safety and health and hoped he would soon return to resume the medical research he'd already been doing at a family friend's lab. His father often tried to telegraph him money, which he always refused, sometimes angrily. It is clear that he believed if he didn't intend to go along with his parents' dream of a safe professional future, he should make his way on his own. His letters home were filled with allusions to monumental events—with which he was increasingly associated in some way—and dry wit and cryptic descriptions of what and how he was doing at the time of writing, usually much too cryptic and unorthodox to put the letter's recipient at ease.

In one such letter from Guatemala to his favorite aunt, Beatriz (dated July 22, 1954), he describes with his characteristic mix of wry humor and great perspicacity the overthrow of the Jacobo Arbenz[2] government:

> Here it was all great fun with shots, bombardments, speeches and other events, which interrupted the monotony in which I lived. I will be leaving in a few days, I don't know how many, for Mexico, where I intend to make a fortune selling whalebones for shirt collars. In any case, I will be on the alert to go to the next flare-up, since there certainly will be one, because the Yankees cannot live without defending democracy somewhere or other.

Che's often self-mocking humor is already in evidence. And along with his teasing jocularity—this aunt was famously anticommunist—Che's astute and ironic observation about the Yankees not being able to live without defending democracy somewhere or other continues to ring true half a century later.

One of the things this book makes clear is Guevara's profound interest in the sites of ancient civilizations; wherever and whenever possible he visited the great Inca and Mayan ruins of Peru, Guatemala, and Mexico. This early passion resonates deeply with me, and the wanderer writes with great knowledge, sensibility, and delicious detail. But in another letter, this one written in May 1954 responding to one from his mother, in which she allows herself to ask about his future plans, he says:

> It is improbable that anthropology should become the only occupation of my mature years. . . . The idea of investigating that which is dead beyond repair, as the aim of my life, seems a bit paradoxical.

I am sure of two things. The first is that if I reach an authentically creative stage by around thirty-five, my exclusive — or at least main — activity will be nuclear physics, genetics or some area of that sort, which brings together the most interesting aspects of the subjects I know. The second is that our America will be the scene of my adventures in a much more important way than I could have imagined. I feel that I have really learned to understand it, and I feel American, from that America whose character is distinct from all other peoples of this earth.[3]

Che would not become a geneticist or nuclear physicist, although like many brilliant people he continued to read in many disciplines and used what he found in them to inform his thinking. On the other hand, his life would indeed unfold to reflect the second affirmation. He was quintessentially American (in the broad, continentally inclusive sense of the term).

Another important source of our insights about the early political development of this man who was to gain such international stature is *My Life with Che*, written by Guevara's first wife, the Peruvian economist and revolutionary Hilda Gadea.[4] It is a self-effacing and moving book, filled with history and anecdotes that bring alive not only the daily lives of the young couple and their friends at the time, but also the great events in which they would become major protagonists. Writing retrospectively, Gadea does not hide her disappointments or stoicism. Neither does she idealize Guevara. Her Andean reserve takes hold, and she calmly recites factual revelations that become windows through which the reader is able to deconstruct much of what was important to the hero during the years they were together. Gadea writes:

On our first meeting, Guevara made a negative impression on me. He seemed superficial, egotistical, and conceited. . . . Later I learned that [he] hated to ask for favors, and that at the time I met him he was suffering from an incipient attack of asthma. These attacks forced him to raise his chest in an awkward position in order to regulate his breathing.

And again:

Like many Latin Americans, I tended to mistrust Argentineans, first because they are often so intent on showing that their country is more developed than the rest of the continent, and second because they have a reputation for being overconfident about their own abilities. However, Guevara's personal qualities soon led me to overcome these prejudices.

The foregoing passages are from Gadea's initial descriptions of Guevara when they met in Guatemala City. In the introduction to her memoir, which attempts an overall evaluation of the man, she writes:

Ernesto Guevara, with his aristocratic family background and his medical degree, could have become a favored son among the elite families in his country—he was gifted enough, intelligent, congenial, cultured. He could have been "successful" in the capitalist style: money and connections. But he eschewed those possibilities in order to contribute directly to the betterment of our lives. And later, as a minister of state and already proven revolutionary, he abandoned that position of power to keep on fighting for the rights of our people. Fully aware of the difficulties ahead, he knew that he could die in the effort, and that his death would not be in vain.

Hilda and Ernesto were falling in love. Yet she clearly understood their class and cultural differences. When she speaks of "our lives," she identifies herself with Latin America's poor Indians and workers of the countryside and cities. Although highly educated, she is from the quiet, reserved background of those indigenous to the Peruvian Andes. Guevara, more European of origin, light-skinned and from a more privileged social class, had to show his commitment through his choices and action, which he did to an extraordinary degree.

Gadea, again in her introduction, sums up the essential Che: "He is neither divine nor a myth, but a revolutionary who evolved day by day, an example for the young generations of the Americas and the world."

Che's mother, Celia de la Serna, was the deeper parent, the more complex of the two. She adored her son and had a special relationship with him. As is true of so many political activists, the son radically changed his parents' lives. In his father's case, the influence was more public and, until late in the older man's life, probably not as profound. But in his mother's, Che's leadership role in the Cuban revolution and his subsequent revolutionary stature led her to assume Left positions with a profound conviction and consciousness of what she was defending and why.

During the Dirty Wars in Latin America's Southern Cone, Che's positions often created problems for his family. But his politics also had a profound effect on his parents and siblings. His oldest brother, Roberto, was certainly radicalized by Che and later in his life became involved in progressive politics. A younger brother, Juan Martín, followed in his famous sibling's footsteps. He founded an Argentinean revolutionary organization, and as a result he spent many years in prison. His sister Celia, about whom I write at the beginning of these notes, lived in Europe for a while; there she worked tirelessly for Juan Martín's release. Now she is back in Argentina. Another sister, Ana María, lived in Cuba until her early death from cancer. There was also Aunt Beatriz, with whom Che always maintained a close relationship. She followed her favorite nephew's adventures closely, and when he was murdered she resolutely refused to accept the news—or to speak his name again.

Che's mother, Celia, went to prison once for several months as a result of her son's notoriety. Already incommunicado on distant shores during the Congo campaign, and aware that the probability of his survival was less than 50 percent, he wrote moving farewell letters to his wife, children, and family in Argentina. Sadly, his mother died a month before her son's last letter arrived.

From correspondence that exists from mother to son as well as from son to mother, we get a sense of the extraordinary bond between the two. It was a political as well as maternal bond. Because he was in Congo at the time of her death, Che received the news long after the fact. He wrote "The Stone," one of his few short stories, out of the pain her loss engendered. Days before her death, Celia still hoped to hear from her firstborn. It wasn't to be. At her funeral, Che's picture rested on his mother's coffin. A daughter-in-law has said she believes her other children felt left out.

Che got much of his intelligence, conviction, strength, and tenacity from his mother. In her own way, and in her time and place, she consistently made choices of which she—and he—could be proud.

chapter nine
che and fidel

Among the evidence that has led some to claim that Fidel Castro disengaged with Che's final guerrilla efforts, there remains the way he handled the farewell letter Che gave him before he left the country. Several historians insist that this document, in which the warrior said goodbye to the statesman to whom he had been close for so long, was not to be made public unless and until Che died in combat. Guevara disappeared from public life around the end of March 1965. He would fight in Congo and Bolivia before his death more than two years later. Yet Fidel read his letter at the presentation of Cuba's new Communist Party Central Committee on October 3, 1965.

In the missive, Che relinquished his Cuban citizenship, membership in the Cuban Communist Party, government posts, and all that linked him to the Cuban revolution. He remembered when and where he and Fidel met, declared that his dying thought would be of his friend, and said his only regret was not having recognized sooner the Cuban's great leadership qualities. He also said that he was leaving nothing material to his wife and children and that this didn't concern him because he knew the revolution for which he

Fidel Castro and Che Guevara in the
Sierra Maestra during the Cuban war, 1950s.
Photographer unknown.

had fought would give them everything they needed to grow and make their own contributions.

If Che had really intended that this letter not be made public until his death, some analysts argue, then the fact that Fidel read it to the Cuban people so long before points to a rupture of sorts, or at least implies that the Cuban president now saw the Argentinean in a different political sphere.

He was in a different political sphere, but one I still believe was essentially supported by the Cuban revolution. Che was in Congo; he hadn't yet embarked on his Bolivian campaign. Fidel's reading of this letter effectively made it impossible for him to return to Cuba. He did come back for a brief time, on Fidel's urging, physically altered and in complete secrecy, only to train and gather the guerrilla force he would take with him to Latin America.

A secondary effect of the letter's publication was to rob Che of the identity he shared with the other Cuban soldiers fighting alongside him in Congo. Having formally broken with their country, he no longer possessed the authority he'd once commanded. A legal and even to some degree cultural breach was created, which Che alludes to in his Congo diary.

One possible explanation for Fidel having read the letter at this particular moment was that he felt he had to get rid of Che, and this was how he accomplished that. There was no violent fight, as has so often been suggested by counterrevolutionaries and others on the Right. Much less would Fidel have murdered his old friend and comrade. But this was precisely the problem: extraordinarily weighty and impossible to resolve either by those grotesque scenarios put forth by the revolution's detractors or by Cuba's openly continuing to support liberation struggles in other lands.

Another explanation, and one I believe more plausible, is that with the establishment of Cuba's Communist Party and the consequent public announcement of those on its Central Committee and Politburo, some reason had to be given for Guevara's absence. For a while now, he had not been seen in public. His government positions had been taken over by others. Rumors certainly abounded as to why this might be. But in the context of the First Party Congress, conjecture was no longer good enough. Fidel said he felt he had to tell the Cuban people why their beloved Che was not being named to a leadership position. In his mind, reading the farewell letter could no longer be delayed.

There is another, less frequently referenced moment, also involving Fidel Castro, that I believe sheds light on Guevara's character and role in worldwide revolution. This was when, on October 15, 1967, Fidel made his lengthy appearance on Cuban television to confirm Che's death. Global news sources had announced Che's demise many times before, in circumstances that went from believable to bizarre. Now rumors had raged for six days, provoked by news releases from the United States, Bolivia, Europe, and elsewhere, and pulled this way and that by the Cuban people, whose emotions and need to know were running raw.

Members of the Cuban leadership had waited out those six days, examining evidence and considering sources, wanting to make sure of their heart-wrenching conclusions before they presented them in detail to the nation. Che's brother Roberto, representing his Argentinean family, had traveled to Bolivia to identify the body. He had been unable to see it and thus didn't feel he could conclude with certainty that Che was dead. Fidel wanted to respect the family's feelings in this regard. But after examining all the evidence, he believed that it was conclusive and that he could no longer remain silent.

In his TV appearance, the old comrade-in-arms moved slowly and deliberately. He discussed photographs, excerpts from the last entries in Che's combat diary, contradictions and certainties. After demonstrating, without question, that the sad news was true, he went on to make a distinction I think important in analyzing Che's temperament and even shedding some light on why he may have taken chances that—at least in retrospect—seem so ill-advised.

Fidel reminisced in a series of stories about Che's participation in Cuba's war of liberation. He referred to numerous occasions on which the guerrilla leader himself had gone out at the head of a scouting mission or had exposed himself on the front lines of battle when a more careful commander would have issued orders from the rear:

> We must say that we were always worried about the possibility that this temperament, this ever-present bravado of his in moments of danger, could lead to his death in virtually any battle. No one could ever be sure he would adopt even minimal caution or security measures. . . .
>
> On the other hand, he was highly conscious of the importance of the mission he had taken on. And it is possible that he was thinking, as he always did, of the relative value of individuals and the incomparable value of example. This was part of his personality. We would have liked nothing more than for him to have become the protagonist of great people's victories rather than an architect of future victories. But a person of that temperament, personality, and character, of that way of consistently reacting to specific circumstances, is unfortunately more likely to become an architect than a protagonist. And yet the architects are obviously also creators of victories—the greatest creators of victories![1]

"The relative value of individuals and the incomparable value of example," "an architect as opposed to a protagonist or creator." Right here we have one of the important distinctions between Fidel and Che. The first was the leader of a nation, the second the guerrilla leader. The first was the creator of a new society, the second the man who hoped to help initiate many such future societies.

Che was the warrior who believed national liberation was possible only through armed struggle, and many times he had made it clear that once the Cuban war was won he intended to lend his military efforts to other peoples of the world. Fidel had, by virtue of necessity, become the statesman—with other commitments, problems, and priorities.

Cuba was being continuously and ferociously attacked by the United States and isolated by every country within the US sphere of influence. Fidel had to design a strategy for his victorious revolution capable of keeping it afloat. The Soviet Union and other socialist bloc countries were increasingly the main diplomatic, trade, and military partners sustaining the vulnerable nation. As head of state, Fidel was forced to make decisions that often conflicted with Che's ideas about how the new society should be structured, as well as with his vision of world revolution.

Fidel Castro is as goal-oriented as Che ever was. When the two men met in Mexico, they immediately recognized each other's brilliance, determination, and unusual leadership skills. The unique aspects of their characters, what brought them together, may eventually also have been what sent them on differing, conflicting paths. But I remain convinced that Fidel loved Che deeply and remained faithful to his old friend and comrade.

After a long illness, at the age of eighty-one, Fidel Castro handed temporary power to his younger brother Raul in mid-2006. Two years later, he resigned his positions as president of the country and head of its Council of State. He said he no longer had the physical ability to lead and indicated that it was time for younger people to step up. To date, no younger leaders have successfully made their appearance. Sadly, I don't believe the Cuban structure has really encouraged them. Raul Castro seems fully in control. In many ways he has continued his brother's policies, but has also proven to be more flexible and open to change.

Fidel has said he only wishes to fight now as "a soldier of ideas." Short ideological pieces periodically appear above his byline in *Granma*, the Communist Party daily. The guerrilla leader turned statesman ruled longer than any other socialist president. He remained a thorn in the side of a long succession of US administrations, but he brought his people a measure of justice: land reform, jobs, free education from kindergarten through university, universal health care, and, perhaps most importantly, dignity.

And I am left with another realization, one that is tangible and decisive. Che died in the prime of his years. His beautiful face, filled with the ecstasy of life—even when odds were that his would be cut dramatically short—accompanies us in multiple images. Fidel has grown old. The once powerful figure is fragile, the brilliant mind only giving off occasional sparks of light. This, perhaps, is what truly separates the two men today.

Haydée Santamaría, Havana, Cuba, 1976.
Photo by Margaret Randall.

chapter ten
che and haydée

Che Guevara and Cuban revolutionary heroine Haydée Santamaría
are linked in ways that may surpass even his deep connections to
Fidel or to his wife and children. They were like siblings or spiritual twins, inhabiting a dimension to which few others have access.
"Without him, I almost cannot imagine the revolution," she once
said.[1] And yet, at a casual glance, they were two people who could
not have appeared more different. Haydée was small, between deli-
cate and plain in appearance. She was slightly hunched, though she
held herself with striking dignity. Che was tall and commanding.
Physically, only their piercing gazes were similar. But they shared a
unique characteristic, more difficult to define than looks.

Haydée Santamaría was of Che's generation; she from the balmy
but hurricane-swept Caribbean island, he from Argentina, a country whose European settlers had a reputation for sophistication and
self-satisfied smarts. Her family was from a provincial sugar mill
town, where the mill owners and laborers lived sharply contrasting lives.[2] She possessed the pride of an islander. His background
was citified and aristocratic but had become what we would call
middle class. He had the Rioplatense's deft way with words, and
something extra. Gender gave them very different childhoods, with

different opportunities and expectations, but neither paid much attention to the social restrictions of their time.

As to their formal educations, she went only as far as sixth grade but seemed to absorb the world as if by osmosis. He finished medical school, was widely read, and enjoyed a luxury of exploration before committing to revolutionary struggle. She was naturally more sheltered in her youth, but didn't hesitate to join a group of underground rebels and participate in a secret military operation against a repressive dictatorship. He traveled Latin America, fought in the Cuban revolution, and, when that war was won, spearheaded economic reform in a country not his own. Then he went on to several other foreign battlefields, eventually surpassing death as a worldwide symbol of rebellion and change.

Her first travels were to buy guns from the Miami mafia. Not until many years later would she journey the world to represent the Cuban revolution. She lived through unspeakable personal horror and loss before imprinting her brilliance and exquisite sensibility on the continent's most innovative and respected arts institution, Casa de las Américas.

When he went off to fulfill his dream of ongoing liberation, Che left five children behind. He knew that his wife would care for them and the revolution would provide a healthy context in which they could grow and flourish.[3] Haydée gave birth to two children of her own—a daughter and son—and adopted more than a dozen orphans whose parents had perished in Latin America's diverse theaters of revolutionary war. Her daughter, Celia Hart, has written: "Year by year my siblings varied in number."[4] She eventually left them all by taking her own life in 1980. Despite these differences—which can be ascribed to culture, gender, and personality—Che's and Haydée's lives came together in a shared history that almost defies description.

Every great movement for social change is made up of many exceptional men and women, people endowed with more than the usual quota of passion, creativity, and courage. Among them there may be one or two—a half dozen at most—who are living examples of that almost otherworldly purity of spirit that speaks of the future we imagine in the here and now we've inherited. In Cuba, Che and Haydée were such people. They are inextricably linked in my sense of what real social change must be: examples of the sort of human being required for such a seemingly impossible undertaking.

Again, Haydée's daughter perhaps put it best when she wrote: "From the moment she saw him, my mother understood Che Guevara's enigma, the unique myth his hopeful image has become for generation after generation. She got it long before he became the Heroic Guerrilla."[5]

One of only a very few women who participated in Fidel Castro's 26th of July Movement from its inception, Haydée belonged to the brave group that attacked Moncada Barracks on July 26, 1953, and that would later adopt that date as its name.[6] Her brother Abel was Fidel's second in command. Her lover at the time was also involved. Both of these men were captured and brutally tortured to death by Batista's soldiers, losses that marked her profoundly.[7] Haydée and Melba Hernández survived that failed attack and did prison time, as did Fidel and most of the others who managed to make it out alive.

The Moncada action, although a military failure, is credited with having launched the Cuban revolution. In 1956, following amnesty and Fidel's exile to Mexico—where he and Che met—the rebels returned and regrouped in the mountains of eastern Cuba. Haydée was a leader in the urban underground and also became an important liaison, leaving and entering the country to secure money and arms. She often came and went from the rebel headquarters deep in the Sierra Maestra.

Haydée's and Che's friendship was forged in those dramatic times. A successful insurgency depends on absolute discretion. Death is a constant. Commitments are made quickly and fully; one never knows what the next day or even the next hour will bring.

Comrades develop relationships that endure: some of these are romantic in nature, some familial, and some involve mentorship; others inhabit a category of their own, one for which we have no descriptive term.

In Cuba, the generation that won the war enjoyed a special position, including a trust that crossed lines of class, race, even gender. The heroes morphed into examples. The men wore long hair and beards and sported bright strings of Santería beads until a couple of years after the war ended, when a sort of puritanical ethic set in and Fidel alone kept the beard. Che didn't have a lot of facial hair, although he wouldn't have been one to adhere to an arbitrary dress code in any case. At the end of his life, of course, photographs reveal the now-famous image of a man with long, battle-weary hair and a beard ragged from combat.

The women who took part in Cuba's war of liberation necessarily conformed to the changing social standards differently from the men. As the 1950s came to a close, modesty was still a virtue. In the 1960s, while young men and women in the United States shouted their nonconformity by wearing their hair long, Cuban youth were encouraged to cut theirs and adhere to more conservative dress. In the country to the north, the government discouraged protest. In the country to the south, the government did as well. The revolution was already beginning to institutionalize, and protest was feared.

Women in Cuba observed the Latin American dress code of the decade: simple outfits, hems below the knee, pants only after voluntary fieldwork became the norm. Revolutionary women tended to think of themselves as models for the younger generations (although the rebels were also mostly quite young). To counteract the wild rumors soon being spread by US intelligence services, about "communists who would steal children from their parents and send them to the Soviet Union" or "revolutionaries who had no morals and indulged in wild sex orgies," the few Cuban women in leadership positions were careful about their appearance and manners.

I have written elsewhere about Haydée. I met her on my first visit to Cuba, in 1967, where her intensity and warmth immediately drew me in. We became friends. Although she was not an artist or writer and had never shown a particular aptitude for intellectual pursuits, creating a new society demanded everyone's efforts. When there was a job to be done, the most likely candidate was recruited, whether or not that person had training or experience.

There is the story—perhaps apocryphal—about a meeting at which someone asked if there was an economist (*economista*) in the room. Che raised his hand because he thought the man had asked for a communist (*comunista*). It is rumored that this is how he became head of the national bank. True or not, the story is indicative of the times.

Haydée may have become director of Casa de las Américas by default as well. She was genuinely interested in people and fascinated by their artistic creations, but had no formal training in art or literature. This was probably a stroke of luck for the institution. She possessed an intensity well suited to engaging with artistic personalities. She understood them, and they felt seen by her. What came through was a simplicity and genuineness that created an immediate bridge. She was nothing less than a genius at the job.

From the moment Fulgencio Batista fled the country and Fidel and his comrades took over, the challenge was to create a new set of social relations, all shoulders to the wheel. The society the young revolutionaries envisioned was one that would be rooted in justice and would do away with the poverty, class divisions, racism, misogyny, and dependence on the United States and the local oligarchy that had frustrated the Cuban people for so long. The leaders of this revolution—Fidel, Che, and Haydée among them—understood that cultural and artistic nourishment was as important as defense, economic growth, and welfare. More than half a century later, this remains one of the revolution's most exuberant and powerful characteristics.

From the beginning, the United States spared no effort in trying to destroy Cuba's new social experiment: through economic, military, and diplomatic measures and by isolating the country from its neighbors and natural allies. The cultural blockade was as insidious as any of the others, and Casa de las Américas was the institution charged with breaking through that particular wall. For more than half a century it has continued to do just that, by bringing artists and writers from Latin America and the world to the island and promoting the work of Cuban artists internationally.

But it wouldn't be just any artistic work. As in most countries at the time, men dominated every genre. Haydée knew that literature, painting, music, theater, and all the other art forms had to be democratized, but she never assumed this meant lowering standards or making the arts easier for the masses to understand. With Fidel, she believed in educating the population so it would be able to appreciate the best art.

Casa's democratization process, though, goes beyond presenting first-rate art to an eager public. It involves encouraging and promoting more women artists, more artists of color, and more artists of different sexual identities. Indigenous artists are now recognized as creators of fine art rather than of mere craft. During Haydée's tenure at Casa this was an organic process, and since her death it has accelerated. Young people, women and men, black and white, gay and straight, head the institution's departments today, while those who remain from its founding generation continue to mentor them. I have often wished that the country's Party and government bureaucracies were as fluid and diverse.

Haydée related to hundreds of artists and writers from almost as many countries and in dozens of genres as if she had known them all her life. And these relationships were profound. She had an instinct for what was authentic, important, and unique, and also for what was lacking, what a person's intimate yearning might be. She listened. She grasped experimentation and new artistic forms. She shunned correct lines.

In the revolution's most difficult periods, when some of Cuba's best creative spirits suffered painful repression or were misunderstood by those in power, Haydée invariably made a place for them. This included important gay artists and anyone who didn't conform to the aesthetic of the moment. Silvio Rodríguez and other members of the New Song Movement were victims of such small minds. Haydée protected them, and as saner heads prevailed they became international stars of the new Cuban revolutionary culture. There are many such stories.

Until her suicide in 1980, Haydée was the spirit behind this ever-expanding network. I will never forget my telephone ringing past midnight one night and the voice on the other end of the wire telling me Haydée was dead. Nor can I abstract myself from the subsequent hours I spent at her wake. We were a nation of mourners crowded together in grief and disbelief. I suppose before getting back to Che, I should say a bit about that suicide, which affected so many of us so deeply. I prefer to quote Haydée's daughter Celia on the subject:

> We have no choice but to respect those who decide they'd rather be dead than alive. . . . I am—or was—her daughter, and she left me here when she died. She left me surrounded by a few other walking dead, but in a world in which Cuba exerts a gravitational and magnetic pull as the epicenter of the people's struggles for a better future. . . . She left me safe and provided for. . . . Our final victory—Yeyé's as well—is contained in the attainment of happiness on a certain blue planet in a solar system within the Milky Way. Perhaps a few centuries from now its inhabitants will say: "Our good fortune may very well be linked to a tiny apartment on a small island on our not-very-large planet. The earth is happy; now we should turn our sights to the sun."[8]

The final sentences quote Haydée herself, speaking about the Havana apartment that belonged to her brother Abel, where Fidel and his group planned the action that would change the course of Cuban history. When Haydée Santamaría took her own life, all sorts of conjecture raged as to why. Her marriage had recently ended, and some said that was the reason. Whatever pushed her over the edge, I have always felt that what figured most prominently in her tragic decision was the accumulated weight of so much personal loss, finally including Che and their dream of Latin American liberation.

This is a book about Che, not Haydée. I have spoken of the women in Che's life: his mother, sisters, wives, daughters, and comrades-in-arms. Che and Haydée weren't blood family. As far as I know they were never lovers. Nor did they share a front-line experience. But the way she spoke about him, publicly as well as privately, exudes something of the mysterious kinship I also feel — admittedly at a much greater remove. Perhaps I think of their friendship as the one I would have wanted had I known Che in life.

Or perhaps it is because I see these two exceptional beings as similar in so many ways. Haydée was one of those rare purists who inhabited her principles completely. She was wildly creative and passionate about everything she did. She believed in the possibility of a new world with a ferocity some might call mad. She and Che shared these qualities, and this clearly enabled them to understand one another at a level few could penetrate or share.

In 1966, Che had returned clandestinely to Cuba. He was secluded at a training camp in the western part of the island and completely removed from the public eye. His physical appearance had been altered so that even someone very close would have had a hard time recognizing him. His wife, one of the few allowed to visit, once brought their oldest daughter, Aleida, and introduced Che to the child as "a friend of your father's." Later the girl confided to her mother: "That man loves me." It was at this camp that

Che wrote a letter to Haydée, addressing her by the endearment those closest to her used:

Dear Yeyé:

Armando [Hart] and Guillermo [García Frías] told me of your troubles. I understand your decision and respect it, but I would have preferred to have hugged you than send this letter. The security precautions during my time here have been very severe, and they have kept me from seeing many of the people I love (I'm not as uncaring as I sometimes seem). I'm experiencing Cuba now almost as if I were a foreigner here on a visit: everything from a new and different angle. And my impressions, despite my isolation, make me understand those impressions visitors take with them when they leave.

I appreciate the medical/literary gifts. I see that you have become a writer with a talent for synthesis, but I confess I liked you best that New Year's day, with guns blaring all around and all your ammunition spent. That image, and our time together in the Sierra—even our fights back then are precious memories—are what I will carry with me for my personal use. The love and determination of all of you will help in the difficult moments to come.

I love you,

your colleague (Ernesto Che Guevara).

I know of another letter from Che to Haydée, written two years earlier (1964). A year before that, Cuba's Union of Writers and Artists (UNEAC) had published his *Pasajes de la guerra revolutionario* (*Passages from the Revolutionary War*), and apparently he had a royalty check due. True to his principles, Che wrote to Haydée:

I told the Writer's Union to return the money to you, leaving written instructions so I wouldn't have to engage in a discussion that might have had larger repercussions for something so unimportant. The bottom line is that I cannot accept a penny from a book that does nothing more than narrate the ups and downs of the war. Do whatever you want with the money.[9]

After consulting with Che about a couple of ideas, she used the income from those royalty payments to establish a prize in his name for young Cuban writers.[10]

When Che was murdered in Bolivia, *Casa de las Américas* magazine dedicated an issue to tributes from around the world. The first of these was a letter from Haydée to her old friend: "Hasta la victoria siempre, Che querido" ("Until Victory Always, Dear Che"):[11]

Che:

Where can I write you now? You would tell me anywhere, to the Bolivian miner, Peruvian mother, guerrilla fighter who is or isn't but will be. I know all that, Che. You yourself taught me, and anyway this letter isn't really for you. How can I tell you that I never cried so much since the night I heard they killed Frank [País]—even though when it was announced I didn't believe you were really dead. We were all sure you were still alive, and I said: "It's not possible, a bullet can't bring down that which is immortal. Fidel and you must live. If you don't, how can we?" Fourteen years ago I saw those die whom I loved most in the world—I think I've already lived too long. The sun isn't any longer so beautiful, the palm trees don't give me pleasure anymore. Sometimes, like now, although I love life so much, knowing it's worth opening one's eyes each morning if only for those two things, I want to close them forever, like you.

This continent doesn't deserve this, that's the truth. With your eyes open, Latin America would have found its way forward. Che, the only thing that might have consoled me would have been to have gone with you. But I didn't go. I'm here with Fidel. I have always done what he wanted.

Do you remember? In the Sierra you promised. You said: "You won't miss the coffee, we'll drink mate." You were an internationalist, borders didn't exist for you, but you promised you would send for me when you were finally in your Argentina. I never doubted you would keep that promise. Now it cannot happen, you couldn't, I couldn't.

Fidel said it, so I know it's true. How sad. He couldn't say "Che." He drew on all his strength and said "Ernesto Guevara." That's how he broke the news to the people, your people. What tremendous sadness. I cried for the people, for Fidel, for you, because I can't take it anymore. And later, at your wake, when our great people wondered what rank Fidel would confer upon you, he said "artist." I felt that any rank would have been too low, inadequate, and Fidel as always found the right one.

Everything you created was perfect. But you created something unique: yourself. You showed us that a new human being is possible. Everyone could see that this new being is real, because he exists, he is you.

What more can I say, Che? If only I knew how to speak like you did. Once you wrote me:

I see that you have become a writer with a talent for synthesis, but I confess I liked you best that New Year's day, with guns blaring all around and all your ammunition spent. That image, and our time together in the Sierra— even our fights back then are precious memories—are what I will carry with me for my personal use.

That's why I can't write about you, and you will always have that memory.

Until victory always, dear Che,
Haydée.

Celia Hart says that on hearing the news of Che's death, her mother was inconsolable. Inconsolable and angry: "What a machista, what an outrageous machista! He promised he would take me with him to make the revolution in the rest of America. He promised but he went without me."[12]

The word-for-word transcription of Che's memory in Haydée's farewell letter creates an echo that projects a connection beyond those achieved in most relationships. A heartbeat of mutual sorrow and hope permeates every line.

Haydée Santamaría would live thirteen years past writing this farewell, every minute of that time borrowed against a calendar already spent.

chapter eleven
exercising power, exercising solidarity

Despite my profound admiration, there are a number of things that have disappointed me about Fidel Castro over the years, most importantly his overlong tenure in office. The Cuban Communist Party has failed to allow younger generations of revolutionary cadre to take the reins of the Party or state, refused to open the political process to competing ideas. I am not advocating here for a US-style democracy, which is not the model to which I would aspire. Rather, I would look for inspiration to some of the many other democratic models throughout the world, from the Netherlands to Canada to Uruguay to South Africa.

Ultimately, of course, Cuba has the right to develop its own model, free from outside interference. I respect this right and have been consistent in my opposition to the US blockade and all other attempts to invade the country's sovereignty. What troubles me is what I perceive as stagnation, an unshakable retention of power, on the part of a closed leadership circle, a rigidity that prevents a plurality of ideas on the part of the Cuban people themselves. While during the revolution's early years almost every Cuban on the island held Fidel in extraordinary esteem, in the period leading up to his handing the reins to his younger brother many had begun

Aleida and Che disguised as
Josefina and Ramón, Tanzania, 1965.

to feel he had lost touch with ordinary citizens and their needs. Preventing renovation and renewal is never healthy.

In Fidel's early tenure as leader of the Cuban people, he was a force of nature: a great teacher with an extraordinary vision, capable of orchestrating one of the most important social experiments of the second half of the twentieth century. I remember his early speeches, many of which I was privileged to attend, as brilliant lessons in history or economics. He would move from the general to the particular and back again until everyone present not only understood what he was saying but could also see how it affected his or her life. He was never condescending, always passionate but respectful.

But we have seen how keeping power in the hands of a small group of men can retard a nation's development and a people's freedom. We see this in Cuba itself and in Nicaragua, among a number of other countries. Despite my admiration for much of what has been done in Venezuela, Chavez's strongman image also worries me. In Cuba, when people speak about Che one has the sense they keep him close as a symbol of a less dogmatic style of leadership, or one entirely devoid of subterfuge. How much of this impression reflects the hero's character and how much may be due to the fact that he died so early is difficult to access. He is frozen in perfection.

Returning to Che and Fidel, it must have been unbelievably difficult for the latter to leave his old comrade-in-arms adrift. But once Che insisted on moving on to other battlefields, this may have been exactly what he was forced to do in order to keep the Cuban state alive.

I believe Benigno's failed attempts to get the Cuban leader to talk to him, to answer legitimate questions about what went wrong in Bolivia, can be traced above all to Fidel's internal struggle around promoting "two, three, many Vietnams" in Latin America. Not that many years before, he too had waged war against a dictatorship supported by the most powerful nation on earth. His own dreams of world liberation were no different from Che's. Both men were passionate, committed, arrogant, impulsive, ready at all times to fight for what they believed. How to reconcile the fact that their responsibilities were now so different?

In fact, these differing roles may have been impossible to reconcile. Still, I believe that when it came to Che, Fidel did everything he could to support his old friend's efforts. He tried to get him to wait until better conditions could be achieved. He couldn't convince him to alter his plans. Their visions remained the same. I cannot begin to imagine the anguish their contrasting responsibilities must have caused both men.

There is so much about Cuba that has remained hidden from the US public over these many decades. The country has continued to defend the liberation of all peoples from the exploitation brought on by neocolonialism and imperialism. In international forums its leaders stand up for national sovereignty, independence for the global South, forgiveness of punishing debt, and homegrown solutions rather than those imposed by the North's vested interests. Despite its own considerable problems, the country has consistently shown internationalist generosity to nations that have suffered natural disasters, been engaged in unequal wars of liberation, or simply asked for the help of Cuba's teachers, doctors, and experts in a range of fields.

Over the years, Cuba has taken in thousands of children and educated them at no cost to their home countries. For decades Isle of Youth (formerly Isle of Pines) was filled with special schools, each with five to eight hundred students from a dozen different countries. Attentive to issues of cultural chauvinism, the Cubans even hired teachers from those countries, preserved national customs, and as far as possible replicated the foods those students would have eaten at home. These schools existed for almost half a century, until the last one closed in 2012.

Cuban internationalists have died by the dozens and hundreds and thousands in Nicaragua, the Dominican Republic, Grenada,

Chile, Angola, Ethiopia, Namibia, Guinea-Bissau, and Mozambique, to name just a few of the countries that have requested the revolution's military assistance. Cuba's involvement was key in South Africa's victory over apartheid. Helping struggling liberation movements has continued to be important, and training, arming, and funding those efforts are logical extensions of that commitment. Fidel was as much an architect of these policies as Che was.

But by the time Che took his guerrilla force to Bolivia, Fidel's Cuba was deeply indebted to the Soviet Union, whose strategy included the smaller country providing raw materials for the socialist camp rather than industrializing, which might have improved its economy and enabled it to gain greater independence. The Soviets were willing to aid revolutionary movements in postcolonial Africa, but wanted the Latin American Communist Parties they controlled to call the shots on that continent. They expected Fidel to go along with them. And I suspect that he did his best to lead them to believe he was doing just that.

Che, especially during his tenure as minister of industry, studied the economics of a largely agricultural society. He knew industrialization and diversification were key and advocated for both. Trips to the Soviet Union allowed him to perceive that country's over-centralization and excessive bureaucracy, and he considered these detrimental to healthy growth. He grew closer to the recipe Mao was pushing in China.

This is not the place, nor do I have the economic expertise, to analyze China's solutions with regard to the needs of much smaller Cuba. I will, however, throw out two issues worth thinking about. One is the obvious fact of China's size. That country is the largest in the world, reducing its usefulness as a model for the tiny island nation. The second concerns the mid-twentieth-century socialist camp rivalry between China and the Soviet Union; following one country's model in whatever partial or limited way necessarily created conflict with the other.

For anyone who has studied Cuba around the time of its country's First Party Congress and the establishment of its first Central Committee and Politburo, it is clear there was a clash between those who favored the Soviet line and those who, like Che, saw stagnation in that line. Massive investment was allowing the Soviet Union to win its battle in Cuba. Important decision-making positions began to be filled by pro-Soviet cadre, many of them former members of the country's prerevolutionary pro-Soviet People's Socialist Party (PSP). Independent thinkers such as Che became problematic. The forces that had gained control could get rid of most of these simply by replacing them with people who would toe the new party line. But Che was always independent-minded, larger than life, and beloved to the point of hero worship. One way to remove his internal influence was to support his desire to travel to other lands that demanded his "modest efforts." Che's departure, first to Africa and then to Bolivia, coincided with these events.

We can find support in this history, and also some evidence of ambivalence or hesitancy. It is clear that Fidel was less than forthcoming with the Soviets and the world when he continued to throw Cuba's resources behind a number of revolutionary movements. Such activities by their very nature demand discretion. And he was forced to juggle the aid he needed from the socialist camp with his belief that successful revolutions had an obligation to support liberation struggles in other lands.

Fidel encouraged the preparation of a strong contingent of able men and women who would make up the Bolivian guerrilla force, just as he had with other liberation projects. He personally visited training camps and had innumerable documented meetings with revolutionaries from other countries, trying to judge their seriousness and possibilities of success. The Cubans put a whole governmental department in charge of these preparations, provided logistical attention, created hundreds of false travel documents, and routed the soldiers around the world to their clandestine destinations.

But in Bolivia those soldiers found themselves in a barren region, without the Bolivian Communist Party's promised rearguard infrastructure or adequate communication equipment, and contact with Havana was also finally severed. Some of these problems were undoubtedly due to the stress endemic to this type of irregular warfare. Some must be attributed to Che himself, who had seen the Bolivian campaign through too rosy a lens, one where romanticism and sheer force of will bested clear-headed analysis. Some may be traced to Cuba. I personally have a number of unanswered questions about the role of Manuel Piñeiro, the revolution's top intelligence officer, whose job it was to coordinate the complex insurgency network.

I also want to talk about the essence of failure. It's hard to imagine, when contemplating someone of Guevara's brilliance, sensibility, and experience, why he would embark on such obviously risky missions as those in Congo and Bolivia. In the former, he was a white man with no knowledge of the languages or tribal cultures of the black revolutionaries alongside whom he intended to fight. These people understandably resented him. He also had little verifiable intelligence about the war, because the situation he encountered was untenable beyond his wildest dreams. Bolivia is a Latin American country bordering Che's own Argentina (where he hoped to end up), but there too he found himself in a situation very different from what he expected. The area was inhospitable, the local population sparse and indifferent, the languages and customs problematic.

For all his brilliance, Che failed in Bolivia. And he failed dramatically, to the point of his own demise. Numerous circumstances contributed to this failure, of course, as discussed above. But Che's arrogance and overconfidence clearly played a role, as did an authoritarian leadership model that might have benefited from critique and reassessment.

Che's personal characteristics are part of what it has historically meant to be a great man. They are not simply anomalies that led to his tragic death in Bolivia, but inherently flawed attributes of a classic notion of leadership that he and men like him personify. We, who love the man for many of his other qualities, may be so dazzled by his capabilities that we fail to recognize those places where the arrogance and energy of exceptionality kept him from invoking ordinary common sense.

chapter twelve
the question without an answer

I have been privileged to know a number of extraordinary human beings. I'll mention the abstract expressionist painter Elaine de Kooning; the French-Mexican archeologist Laurette Séjourné; Latin American revolutionaries such as Haydée Santamaría, Roque Dalton, José Benito Escobar, and Dora María Téllez; and US poets Adrienne Rich and V. B. Price. That's the short list.

There are others I haven't known personally, but they too have been among the visionaries of my time: Ho Chi Minh, Albert Einstein, Fidel Castro, Nelson Mandela, and Aung San Suu Kyi, to begin with. And before my time, but continuing to exert a powerful influence, thinkers such as Socrates, great leaders such as Tupac Amaru, scientists such as Galileo and Darwin, composers such as Bach and Mozart, the Peruvian poet César Vallejo, and the gloriously multifaceted Leonardo da Vinci.

These men and women spoke truths difficult for others to understand. They stood up for what they believed and generally didn't suffer fools easily. Each changed the nature of the field in which he or she worked. Every one of them had contradictions, some to such an extent that their contemporaries considered them outrageous or mad. Moving against the current or being markedly

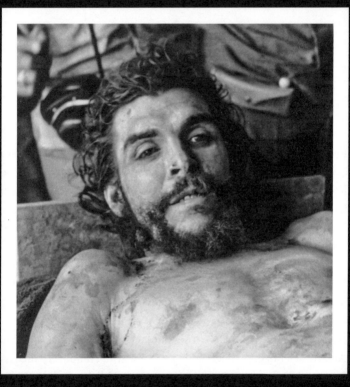

Che Guevara dead, schoolhouse at
Vallegrande, Bolivia, October 9, 1967.
Photo by Freddy Alborta.

ahead of one's time is often misunderstood, or worse. Yet all these people made the world and the way we think about the world forever different.

I place Che Guevara in such a category. As with all these friends, mentors, and heroes, I perceive their lives through a feminist lens. I am careful to situate them in the culture of their times, but their relationship to power is key to how I look at each.

And what about this recurrent idea of failure? Failure too may lead to success. Che's guerrilla effort in Bolivia ended in defeat; there's no question about that. And when some of the survivors joined others to go back and try again, they failed as well. But perhaps it is our notion of time that is skewed. Four decades later, Bolivia has one of the most interesting and innovative progressive governments in Latin America. It didn't appear out of nowhere. There is a continuum from the great nineteenth-century liberator Simón Bolívar, to the revolution of 1952, to the powerful miners' movement of the mid-1960s, to Che's guerrillas at the end of that decade, to Inti Peredo's subsequent effort, and to the nation headed by Evo Morales today.

In reference to Che, Fidel cited "the relative value of individuals and the incomparable value of example."

Failure itself may be relative.[1]

Che knew this.

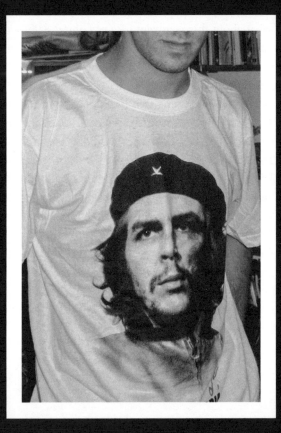

Young man wearing Che T-shirt, Montevideo,
Uruguay, 2011. Photo by Margaret Randall.

chapter thirteen
war and peace

What about war itself? War as a solution to pernicious inequality at home, or invasion by a foreign force?

At this point I am about to take that proverbial leap from the comfort of a lifelong cliff. Looking at Che Guevara's life, I feel I must take a few moments to consider the question of war per se, including armed struggle and the use of violence to bring about a more just society—presumably one that will itself be free of violence.

Che personifies wars of liberation. For much of my life I distinguished between expansionist wars, uninvited and unwarranted invasions of other lands to benefit the invading nation, and people's wars in defense of their own sovereignty. The latter usually involved armed struggle as a means through which victims might confront their victimizers, occasionally even winning. I believed, with Che, that armed struggle was the only way for exploited populations to gain freedom.

As I age, though, I find that my understanding of violence deepens. And my abhorrence of it does as well. Although I continue to stand by my defense of many of the armed movements with which I have had personal experience, and I may again support armed struggle when all other routes have been exhausted, I no longer consider any sort of violence easily defensible. For those of us who have seen or experienced war up close, this may be a logical development. And I have also come to understand that the means tend to vitiate the end—that is, that a struggle waged through the force of arms too often produces a new social structure plagued by the violence of unequal power relations.

I am not alone. Many who share my political persuasions detest war. We have seen its ravages and broken promises. We have learned, painfully, that it rarely brings lasting peace. Even among those who hold opposing views, war for its own sake is losing ground. Colonel Gian P. Gentile, the director of West Point's military history program and commander of a Baghdad combat battalion in 2006, has stated unequivocally that in his opinion the United States gained little after a decade in Iraq and Afghanistan. In the context of a discussion among West Point faculty on the merits of war, Gentile summed it up: "Certainly not worth the effort. In my view."[1]

Governments continue to go to war in defense of all sorts of economic and/or geopolitical interests. Soldiers, often very young ones, predominantly men and women of color and the poor, become the inevitable cannon fodder in such conflicts. Service to country is lauded as an irreproachable reason to fight, no matter that our country may not even be under attack by the nation against which we launch the full power of our sophisticated arsenal.

Economic or geopolitical interests are almost always the real motivators in such conflagrations. Patriotism is stretched out of shape to fabricate a justification for unjustifiable action. Here in the United States, for example, even with regard to two extremely unpopular wars, an outpouring of gratitude to those who fight them is encouraged at every turn. I am always conflicted about this. I feel sympathy for the individual soldier, although I cannot agree with the wars themselves. Part of me is tempted to whisper, "Thank you for your service," even though I am convinced these men and women have been coerced or forced into playing sacrificial lambs.

In times of unending conflict, the heroic image overrides meaningful critique. Years later, pundits and historians may still be arguing about whether or not such wars were worth the terrible loss in human life, the huge numbers suffering from PTSD, the devastation of cultural patrimony, and the irreparable damage to the aggressor's moral stature.

For several generations, Che has been the most recognizable symbol of armed struggle and of the unequal battle of an individual's fearless defense of his or her ideals of equality and justice pitted against state oppression and control. Young people throughout the world—none of them even born when Che lived—who wear the T-shirts and mouth the rhetoric see his legacy as one to be emulated. Depending on where these youths live, the cultures they inhabit, and the values they inherit, the message they absorb may range from simple nonconformity with social hypocrisy to a complex recipe for social change. Whatever the type or degree of influence, Che exemplifies taking power through the force of arms.

At a more sophisticated level as well, Che represented and still represents the armed struggle option. Following the Cuban revolution's success, theorists worldwide discussed the best ways to create other anticapitalist, anti-imperialist societies. Cuba enjoyed a well-earned legitimacy in these discussions; its Tri-Continental Conference, held in Havana in January 1966, provided a venue for debate among the peoples of Asia, Africa, and Latin America who longed to escape domination by the United States or (to a lesser degree) the Soviet Union. The range of Latin American Communist Parties, unions, worker and peasant movements, and student and other organizations intent on promoting social change often espoused contrary points of view. But Cuba, by virtue of having waged a successful revolution ninety miles from US shores, was considered by many to be the voice of authority.

The Tri-Continental Conference was only the most recent in

a series of such gatherings, at which Third World leaders aimed to chart a path clear of the two superpowers. The Bandung Conference had taken place in 1955. Such meetings eventually helped establish the important Non-aligned Nations movement. The Havana conference also launched *Tri-Continental Magazine*, a journal that would feature its ideology in years to come.

Che was not physically present at that conference; he was already waging armed struggle in other lands. But his message to the conclave, read at its closing session, sums up its goal and his. Following a careful and detailed summary of current situations of imperialist domination and consequent misery throughout the developing world, as well as a rundown of popular uprisings against that domination and misery (including serious consideration of the fact that the brutality of war may be avoided in some circumstances), he ends with the oft-quoted paragraph:

> Our every action is a battle cry against imperialism, and a
> battle hymn for people uniting against the great enemy of
> mankind: the United States of America. Wherever death
> may surprise us, let it be welcome, provided that this, our
> battle cry, may have reached some receptive ear and another
> hand extend itself to wield our weapons and other men be
> ready to intone the funeral dirge with the staccato singing of
> the machine-guns and new battle cries of war and victory.

A greater praise song to defiance and war can hardly be imagined. Targeting the United States as mankind's greatest enemy was certainly reasonable. From the Cuban revolution's earliest days, the country to the north had launched diplomatic and economic blockades, prevailed upon those nations in its sphere of influence to break relations with Cuba, tried outright invasion (Bay of Pigs) and covert crop plagues and assassination attempts. Revolutionary rage was understandable. But with its emphasis on welcoming death wherever it surprises us, and its intoning the machine-gun staccato along with the funeral dirge, Che's message also glorified death, as long as that death came in the process of seeking liberation.

Revolutionaries of the 1970s and 1980s, including Che, often emphasized that they were fighting for life, not death. Still, they died by the thousands, and killed many. Most differentiated themselves from traditional military forces by following a code that kept innocent death to a minimum. But little beyond the rhetorical has been written about the human cost of revolutionary war. It is as if its nature renders it immune.

I've already spoken about the *foco* theory, the idea that a small group of armed guerrillas in concert with impoverished people who have nothing to lose but their misery and hopelessness may be capable of occupying territory and establishing a beachhead from which to wage a successful war of liberation. Che became the activist, the idealized example of this theory, and the French journalist Régis Debray its principal theoretician.

Leaders of revolutionary movements throughout history have almost always tried legal or democratic means of changing society before going to war. Armed struggle has been a last resort except for some of the more criminally belligerent organizations, such as Peru's Shining Path, or The Lord's Resistance Army, which has wreaked such havoc in northern Uganda, South Sudan, the Democratic Republic of Congo, and the Central African Republic. The use of child soldiers in such armies further differentiates them from the more legitimate organizations and has shown their utter irresponsibility and perversion.

But even where the most authentic guerrilla movements for change are concerned, governmental control and subterfuge can be overwhelming. Democracy and its much-touted but easily subverted electoral processes, as well as revolutions, have proved easy to disrupt or corrupt. The United States and national oligarchies have invariably been ready with propaganda, manipulation, training, and financial aid. In the last decades of the twentieth century it became a truism that when all other means failed, the force of arms remained viable. The Cuban revolution showed that armed struggle could be successful. And Che Guevara became its standard-bearer.

To those who claim that Left revolutionaries are terrorists, I respond in three ways. First, I question the term, which has been so easily and loosely applied to anyone presumed to be against our national interests or security, without bothering to understand where that person is coming from or what we have may have done to influence his or her position. I speak about how the demonized term has changed here in the United States, from fascist to communist to terrorist—meaning, in my lifetime, from Nazi to Soviet sympathizer to Muslim.

Then I point out that a dictatorial state, because it has such an absolute hold on power, wages its own war of terror through impoverishment, extreme exploitation, layoffs, foreclosures, and inadequate or nonexistent health care and education. Last, I say that with few exceptions the great revolutionaries I have known embody a depth of humanity unimaginable in their opponents.

I will always remember Haydée Santamaría telling me that when she had to send someone out to place bombs or engage in other acts of urban insurgency, she made sure she chose a person she knew would hate the task: "This preserved the lives of innocent people. I didn't want anyone to get used to those operations," she said, "or enjoy them." This, to me, is typical of the revolutionary ethic. It flies in the face of violence for violence's sake.

There are also those who dispense with anything short of armed action as weakness, a position incapable of bringing about change. They see pacifists as too cowardly to fight, or at best irrelevant. Peg Morton of Eugene, Oregon, a longtime Quaker nonviolent activist, has been on the front lines of almost every one of our struggles for decades: against imperialist wars and US government training and financing agents of brutality, against nuclear arms, against poverty, for racial and gender justice, in defense of disability and other rights. At eighty-one, Morton has prayed, stood in, sat in, protested, fasted, accompanied, gone to prison, and, finally, made her life a paean to social change. A staunch pacifist, she is nevertheless practical and thinks about every action in light of how it may advance her goal of justice. Regarding violence, she has written:

> It is better to be violent than passive. The worst attitude, when evil confronts us, is not to face up to it. What is crucial is an unshakable faith in the liberating power of nonviolence and an inexhaustible energy for systematically realizing it. The key elements of active nonviolent struggle are strength and gentleness.[2]

This affirmation puts civil disobedience in a powerful light and challenges the idea that pacifism automatically and in all situations eschews the force of arms.

Prior to the Cuban revolution, there were successful examples of nonviolent roads to greater social justice. Gandhi's India was the most powerful of these. But although Gandhi managed to free his country from colonialist control and caste divisions through nonviolent action, the result fell far short of real equality for all Indians. In the United States, Martin Luther King Jr. and César Chávez are examples of leaders who used nonviolent means to effect social change; their ideas and actions also nurtured the pacifist tradition and made valuable contributions to US social change.

At the same time, history is filled with moments when nothing short of armed action is called for: Spain's Civil War (which, had the rebels won, would have made it much harder for fascism to decimate Europe as it did), the Jewish uprisings in the Warsaw and Vilna ghettoes, Palestine's Intifada, and so many others.

After 1959, a series of armed actions throughout Latin America, inspired by the Cuban revolution, also failed to gain ground. Then, in 1970, the electoral route to socialism was attempted in Chile. Salvador Allende was elected president, and for three promising years the Popular Unity government was able to develop a more egalitarian society. Many of us wondered if a peaceful path to change was possible after all. But the United States, in concert with Chile's own right wing and military, succeeded in destroying that experiment with the same series of covert and overt operations they had previously used to bring down more militaristic efforts. At least as much death descended on the Chilean people as if the Popular Unity government had come to power through the force of arms.

Subsequently, several Latin American nations have tried a variety of bloodless coups or nonviolent roads to social change. The extent to which Venezuela, Bolivia, Uruguay, Argentina, and others will succeed in effecting long-term restructuring remains to be seen. At the same time, in a number of Latin American countries where protracted wars of liberation have taken place—Nicaragua, El Salvador, Guatemala, and Peru, to name a few—their successes and failures continue to unfold.

In Nicaragua a genuine people's revolution won power in 1979 and held it throughout the 1980s. But many of its leaders became corrupt, and the United States was eventually successful in getting the Sandinistas voted out of office. Years later, the strongmen from that movement are back in power, this time via elections. But they are a corrupt version of their former selves. It is hard to think of them as representatives of the genuine movement that once inspired so many. Absolute power, easy rhetoric, questionable methods, and sordid outcomes have muddied the picture, one that would require a whole other essay to analyze. Enough to say here that the honest members of the old Sandinista guard have long since quit the party. Some have created new organizations, such as the MRS (Movimiento de Renovación Sandinista, or Movement for Sandinista Renovation), but they have failed to garner sufficient support.

In the other countries mentioned, degrees of freedom dance uneasily with residual power structures. In many of the nations where dictatorships have been overthrown by one means or another, members of the old guard (including torturers) continue to enjoy power and immunity to punishment. This is also true in the

United States, where the Obama administration has been unwilling to try George W. Bush and members of his inner circle for flagrant and well-documented crimes against humanity.

Still, in the past decade human rights groups have made significant progress. There have been hundreds of cases in which torturers have been tried and, in many instances, convicted. Many of these cases are ongoing. Heads of state are no longer automatically immune from prosecution. Successful court proceedings have been brought against Peru's Alberto Fujimori; Liberia's Charles Taylor; Chad's former dictator, Hissène Habré; and even Chile's Augusto Pinochet, while the United States has preferred a path of "forgive and forget." Amnesties, compensation, forgiveness, and effective memorials all require reassessments of war itself. Decisions reflect how a society views violence. As the policy makers, corporate media, and population reshape what is considered acceptable, reassessments follow.[3]

A decade ago in Liberia, David Crane, prosecutor of the Sierra Leone Special Court, issued a warrant for Charles Taylor's arrest, triggering an international incident with Ghana and leading to negotiations with Nigeria for the dictator's exile. The talks seemed to be at an impasse. Then a group of courageous women decided to try to put an end to decades of bloody civil war by attempting a new modality of struggle. Hundreds of women — mothers, grandmothers, aunts and daughters, Christian and Muslim — came together to demonstrate. Their only weapons were their white T-shirts and moral authority.

As the rebel noose tightened around the capital city of Monrovia and the peace talks threatened to collapse, the women sat firm. They prayed. And then they made a threat of their own. They surrounded the building where the talks were taking place, refused to let anyone in or out, and warned that they would remove their shirts if the male representatives tried to leave without coming to an acceptable agreement. The arrest warrant in conjunction with the women's action led to the desired outcome. Taylor fled the country and Ellen Johnson Sirleaf, Africa's first female head of state, was elected in his place. Since then she has been reelected.[4]

Could it be that this extraordinary action was successful because women are able to think differently about power? It is worth noting that continued warfare did not solve the problem. A whole other model of resistance did.

So the big questions are: Is violence the only viable route to positive social change? Can a culture free of violence be created on the shoulders of a war that leaves death and destruction in its wake? Do the ends justify the means, or can a process in which violence is used to achieve social change ever successfully embrace peace? Even when all else has failed, is war really the answer? There is also the related but different question as to the morality of killing, whatever interests it represents or injustices it is meant to redress.

Looking at Che Guevara in his historical moment and context, it is easy to understand how he came to the conclusion that guerrilla warfare was the only route to justice. He had traveled a continent sacked by a superpower, tightly controlled by its international lending institutions, offended by Eisenhower's forced sterilization policy, and broken by exploitation and hopelessness. He had witnessed firsthand the CIA's defeat of a democratically elected government in Guatemala. He had analyzed other failed chapters in the saga of Latin American liberation. And he had been a protagonist in Cuba's successful revolution. The personification of someone whose actions perfectly matched his ideas, he didn't hesitate to place himself on the front lines. In so doing, he became the symbol of that ideology for generations.

What are our options today?

Can we admire Guevara's commitment, purity, and generosity of spirit, his willingness to place himself at the forefront of his ideas, and still disagree with war as a remedy for wrong?

I believe we can.

As demonstrated by Spain's war against fascism, years of conflict in northern Ireland, World War II (the war that was supposed to end all wars), the US debacle in Vietnam, Israel's long occupation of Palestine, the dirty wars in Latin America, traumatic episodes in Bosnia, Rwanda, and Darfur, and the United States' recent invasive assaults upon Iraq and Afghanistan, it is clear that this answer rarely brings peace.

In some cases guerrilla struggles did light the way and, later and in conjunction with citizen efforts, succeed in deposing dictators and installing more egalitarian processes. In others, moments of brute terror subsided only to linger as unresolved and protracted morasses in which ethnic hatred persists and conflict simmers just beneath the surface of society. With imperialistic wars, such as those waged by the US in Vietnam, Iraq, and Afghanistan, years of decimation and killing have meant devastation for the invaded nations and a different kind of trauma for the invaders. Generational scars, including pandemic PTSD and suicide, and violence of all sorts, may continue to plague any nation that believes it has solved a problem by going to war.

There are instances in which armed struggle was clearly the only recourse: South Africa, for example, where decades of combined armed and civic resistance succeeded in overthrowing the racist horror of apartheid. That country is far from peaceful today, but I don't believe any freedom-loving person would argue that the African National Congress should not have used the force of arms.

On the other hand, we can look to the Zapatistas in the southern Mexican state of Chiapas, who have given the world another model—one not based on the desire to take state power. The Zapatistas have drawn on ancient indigenous forms of consensus and decision making and are developing a new way of looking at the issue of power itself. They have a great deal to teach us about struggle. Perhaps it is the lust for power that is so corrupting and easily corruptible.

Undeniably, different historical moments within different national and cultural contexts permit different processes.

Rather than go off on a tangent about whether irregular war may or may not be necessary in certain circumstances, I am interested in addressing the idea of a symbol of armed struggle itself as a positive image. For years I supported that modus as the only possible methodology by people confronting state control (frequently including state terror). It seemed to me that the naysayers dismissed the hidden warfare that is poverty, hunger, ignorance, and oppression. On the other hand, those arguments made by the devil's advocates, who claim that all terrorisms are equal, also seemed weak or cowardly. I believed that any means necessary was legitimate when combating the warfare of the state.

I still do. My question is: although necessary at times, should war be lauded as the symbol par excellence of social change?

Che Guevara was a man of his time. Caught in the social struggle of his era, he took the route he believed necessary to bringing about change, and he made himself its embodiment. For me, his attraction rests in his unusual ability to do what he believed rather than on his assertion that armed struggle was the only way.

If history teaches us anything, it is that war is not the answer. Not regular war and, except in unusual circumstances, not irregular war either.

So I will take these lines as an opportunity to say that I believe war always has negative consequences. Violence always engenders violence, and the idealization of war impregnates our culture with violence as a positive value. The immense upsurge, over the past several decades, of war games (computerized or not), reality TV in which celebrities go into battle with US military personnel, literature, films, theater, art, song lyrics, biased humor, and other rude cultural manifestations have only succeeded in making violence more commonplace and socially acceptable.

This attitude plays into the sexism and homophobia of our gender- and race-skewed societies. Models of behavior encouraged by our laws and commercial media spawn increasingly violent crimes, both domestic and public. A primitive understanding of our Second Amendment rights protects lax gun laws, and a flippant tolerance for the old adage "Boys will be boys" still explains it all away. Any adult citizen can walk into a gun store in the United States and purchase an assault weapon with firepower far beyond that needed to protect his or her family or to hunt.

Hate-crime legislation has become a relatively recent criminal category and has been adopted in a number of US states as more and more horrific crimes based on misogyny, racism, and homophobia have been perpetrated. In these states, if it can be proven that a violent act meets the criteria of a hate crime, stiffer sentences may be meted out. The extreme verticality of fundamentalist religion, with its wrathful God and male-centered social structure, also aids and abets this violence-ridden culture.

Boys will still be boys, so men will still be men. As feminism allows us to explore the issue of power, our experience teaches us more about how power relationships shape the world in which we live, and skewed power relationships foster so many social ills. History confirms these findings over and over again. As a result, we are able to more deeply appreciate women (and men) who value justice and work in peaceful ways to bring it about.

Feminists, with our developed analysis of power, have had important things to say about the violence of war. In recent years, some of the women who took part in the armed struggle organizations of the 1970s and 1980s have begun to reflect publicly on their experiences. Carmen Castillo, a high-ranking member of the Chilean MIR (Movimiento de Izquierda Revolucionaria, or Movement of the Revolutionary Left) who survived the unequal 1975 battle that took her partner Miguel Enríquez's life, has given years of thought to her own participation in an armed struggle organization and to women's somewhat different view of what it means to carry a weapon:

> We've talked about violence, but not so much about the
> way we women lived our militancy. I've spoken with other

Chilean, Argentinean and Uruguayan women—all of whom were involved in armed struggle—and we've asked ourselves: were our weapons symbols of power, phallic symbols, or was there something unique to the way we women understood and used them? Feminism obliged us to reflect on such things. . . . I don't want to idealize the role of women, because the female torturer tended to be the cruelest, just as the powerless person when he or she acquires a degree of power can be the worst abuser of power. But we also realized that many of us women didn't think of our guns as power symbols. We related to them as necessary to protecting our lives. We refused to view them as powerful in and of themselves.[5]

Che Guevara was surrounded by strong women. His mother was unusual for her time and, as we have seen, extremely influential in his development. An aunt was a lifelong reference. During the Cuban war Che worked with extraordinary women such as Celia Sánchez, Haydée Santamaría, and Vilma Espín. Both his wives were activists first, not women typical of the times who became involved in the struggle through a brother or lover. In his last experience in Bolivia he counted on female comrades such as Loyola Guzmán and Haydée Tamara Bunke. None of these women, however, were feminists, nor did they (that I am aware of) question prevailing gender roles. Haydée Santamaría may have come the closest, but not until long after Che left Cuba.

Another decade would pass before feminism emerged in the urban centers of the developed world, and yet another before its analysis began making itself felt in the developing countries. Even then, women on the Left were among the last to embrace a new understanding of power. Male leadership disparaged feminist resistance and stressed the need for unity. The women's loyalty to their organizations and their need to preserve a unified front with male comrades against a much more powerful enemy, as well as the men's eternal promise that once victory was secured their needs would be addressed, kept them safely in the male-dominated ranks.

If the women around Che didn't question the power structure, or the values inherent in violence and war, Che couldn't be expected to ponder these issues. Few men have taken the lead in such areas.

Had Che lived, he might—or might not—have come to question some of the assumptions considered "natural" in his day (endemic to human nature, rather than socially conditioned). Since he did not, we can only conjecture. Analyzing his thought, I think he might have acquired some understanding of feminism's approach to power. But I believe his chosen milieu and theater of action would have continued to nurture a sensibility that favored male agency, including armed struggle.

Times have changed, and with them our capacity to dissect power, deconstruct violence and war, and draw conclusions for future action.

And so I honor Che not for his example of war but for his unflinching pursuit of justice.

Che, Havana, 1963.
Photo by René Burri.

chapter fourteen
revolution and religion

Why religion? Guevara was a warrior of the Left. He believed in
a socialist state, unaffiliated with any congregation. Yet the way
his myth has been orchestrated and the devotion it inspires can
only be described as religious. Religious as in faith-based, and
religious as in the hierarchical nature of patriarchal institutions:
most modern-day churches. Religious belief is rooted in faith: faith
when confronted with that which we do not understand, faith in
the face of disaster or when contending with the unobtainable.
Problematically, revolution too needs faith and obedience to rally
the great numbers of people required to defend it and undertake
its superhuman tasks.

And faith and obedience need their martyrs and saints. Most
religious doctrines teach that however meager or difficult our
earthly lot, we will be rewarded in an afterlife. Great religious figures exalt the glories of heaven. But in almost all the major religions, political conclaves determined what teachings were to be
handed down and how the Church would implement those teachings. Roman Catholicism's Council of Nicaea (325 AD), summoned
by Constantine, was followed by a number of others, all held to
establish doctrine. Political figures have always been behind such

doctrinal decisions. In other major religions, too, and well into modern times, splits and schisms have been driven by politics. The most powerful faction ends up making the rules, then proclaims them divinely inspired in order to coerce congregants into unquestioned submission to authority.

A considerable degree of violence has always accompanied the implementation of religious doctrine. This fact has been intentionally buried in the shadows of Church history. In revolutionary struggle, too, I believe there are significant problems inherent in following this purely hierarchical, often violent, model. As with institutionalized religion, institutionalized revolutionary parties and movements have too often claimed infallibility, employed repression and murder to vanquish perceived threats, and discouraged any questioning of a political strongman's word.

Faith in revolution assumes that although one generation may not live to see the fruits of progressive social change, future generations should be able to build on our failures as well as our successes, and that our grandchildren will reap the benefits. It may be hard to think of this promise as only or even predominantly religious, because it is not concerned with the divine. It does, however, require suspension of disbelief. Its goal is to change economic, political, and social relations here on earth.

A good friend recently reminded me that Marxism, when it takes root in essentially Catholic countries such as Cuba, also takes on religious trappings.[1] Marx believed in the historical inevitability of communism. But he also observed that we live in prehistory. In his "Eighteenth Brumaire," he wrote: "Men make their own history, but they do not make it as they please; they do not make it under self-selected circumstances, but under already existing circumstances, given and transmitted from the past."[2]

I have often wondered how different the outcome of Che's last struggle might have been had he tried to promote revolution in a country where a majority of the population was composed of nonbelievers rather than one in which so many were possessed by religious superstition.

Thinking of this today, I am reminded of an afternoon in Lima, Peru, at the end of 1973. The coup that overthrew Salvador Allende had taken place on September 11 of that year, and refugees from the extreme repression that followed were beginning to flood across Chile's northern border. I was living in Cuba at the time but had been invited to Peru for three months to work for a research institution sponsored by the United Nations' International Labor Office (ILO) and Velasco Alvarado's progressive government.

Che's first wife, Hilda Gadea, was also in Lima, and we made plans to get together to attend a press conference held by some of the refugees. We met at a prearranged spot and tried to make our way across the city. But our efforts coincided with the Cristo Morado procession, an enormous outpouring of faithful that takes place in Lima every year. Throngs followed the statue of the Christ figure draped in purple cloth. There must have been a hundred thousand people in the street. We quickly realized there was no way we were going to be able to get to our destination, and gave up.

I remember that Hilda and I both commented, at the time, on what this show of fervent religiosity had to say about the viability of revolutionary struggle. In order to reach the masses, we realized, any attempt at social change would have to take people's faith into consideration. I have never forgotten this lesson. Neither did many others throughout the continent. Movements for social change in Nicaragua, El Salvador, Guatemala, Haiti, and Brazil all subsequently involved organized people of faith fighting alongside those who came out of student and union movements or Left political parties.

The overwhelming weight of doctrine has been every bit as important in revolutionary configurations as in religious manifestations. Lenin spoke to the importance of a strong party in organizing and leading political struggle. Fidel Castro and Ernesto

Guevara, in different—sometimes complementary, sometimes seemingly conflicting—ways, have been modern prophets of revolution. And they have been as implacable.

One can hardly imagine a more spectacular saint or martyr figure than Ernesto Che Guevara. Although he himself would have recoiled at the designation and at many of the other myths created about him, in Cuba his exploits are recorded in such a way as to keep the legend alive in an almost sacred space. There is a very fine line between legacy and mythology. In the dazzling display of modern-day sound-bite culture, the two are frequently confused, woven into a single symbol-heavy fabric.

In Cuba alone, there are the magna editions of Che's writings and speeches, excerpts of which dominate billboards and are studied at all educational levels. There is the monument, in Santa Clara, to the famously impenetrable armored train he and his men derailed in the final days of the revolutionary war, clearing the way for his column to advance on the capital. There are those first peso notes, signed simply *Che*, from the time when Guevara was president of Cuba's national bank.

Images of the *guerrillero heróico* are everywhere on the island, including one impressionistic metal cutout many stories tall in Havana's Revolutionary Square.[3] Battered posters of Che adorn the inner and outer walls of people's homes. On my last visit to the country, I saw a man with Che's image tattooed on his chest. There is the necropolis, with its eternal flame, in Santa Clara, where his bones and those of his comrades finally came to rest thirty years after they were murdered and disappeared. And there are Guevara's severed hands, preserved like so many other holy relics around the world.

All of these symbols—beautiful, inspiring, or grotesque—subvert Ernesto Guevara's human dimension. They ignore his progressive but ultimately unpopular decisions at the head of Cuba's Ministry of Industry and its national bank. He worked hard to devise a viable Cuban way out of dependent capitalism, rejecting certain formulas then in vogue in the Soviet-dominated socialist bloc. Long after he left the country to do battle on other revolutionary fronts, many of his ideas were proven to have been correct.

Only by looking as long and hard at revolutionary fanaticism as we look at religious fanaticism can we begin to understand how Che and his myth have been used to inspire hope in the most hopeless of situations and even to stand in for positions he did not hold. I emphasize fanaticism. Che himself did not encourage his myth, any more than Jesus of Nazareth encouraged his. Undoubtedly both men would have hated the ways their stories have been bent to justify a variety of attitudes and acts. Jesus's followers have discouraged independent thought, punished scientific discovery, launched inquisitions, imposed reigns of terror, stifled gender equality, declared whole groups of humans unacceptable, and sexually abused and exploited legions of innocent children.

Faux prophets have achieved power and made great fortunes. Entire populations have been kept in ignorance. And subservience has been encouraged as a positive value, especially for racial minorities and women. Iconic religious as well as revolutionary texts have been taken out of context, misquoted and misunderstood, or modified to fit political ends. No wonder Catholics have been discouraged from reading the Bible. Those who bother to explore its many versions and conflicting translations easily perceive that it is a collection of disparate texts, some written down hundreds of years after the events they describe; that it includes some beautiful literature but responds to political and perhaps even literary selection rather than divine law. Both Jesus and Che would have rejected the rhetoric and the dogma, the ways their words have been interpreted in defense of spurious interests. Certainly the gross commercialism would have repulsed them both.

Where revolution is concerned, it is neither the ideology nor the strategy for social change that is problematic, but the dogmatic follow-the-leader mentality that permeates so many political movements. This is not the primitive Christianity of early Christians, but the authoritarianism of the later hierarchical Church: the prophet and his disciples. In terms of Che's life, what continue to motivate real advocates for social change were the man's consistently principled positions and the way he acted on his beliefs. He was absolutely true to his ideals, regardless of the consequences. Many religious saints have also had such high principles.

Every revolutionary leader has pointed out that winning the war is easy when compared with the ongoing effort required to transform society: its organization, values, and work ethic. Che was famous for his conscientious battlefield demeanor and also for his innovation and example in the subsequent restructuring of the state. His work as minister of industry is worth close examination. Taking those values and that work ethic to other lands proved more complicated. Brilliant and experienced, Che must have known what he was getting into, and the probable fate to which he was leading his followers. But, like the Christ figure, he was incapable of giving up. He marched to his execution as if it had been ordained.

Yet the analogy between religious fanaticism and revolutionary fervor only takes us so far. The first is rooted in revelation and a suspension of disbelief: mysticism. The second should be based on economic and political analysis: science. It proposes to change the relations of production, and the relations among people when these gain control over what they produce and acquire real agency in their lives.

My own history with religion is probably worth mentioning here. My family of origin was not particularly religious. But at the age of eleven, in a new town and desperate for a community of friends, I joined an Episcopal youth group and then its congregation. A brief two years later I realized that, while that church's pomp and ceremony delighted my young sensibility, a philosophy of social change gave me a great deal more to chew on. The latter was ultimately more satisfying and enabled me to flee the institution I had joined much to my parents' chagrin. I think I also must have recoiled at its verticality, although I would not have been able to articulate that back then.

When I remember the incident that provoked the break, I cannot suppress a smile. The church I attended collected weekly donations for foreign missions as well as building maintenance. I had only a vague idea what that congregation meant by missions. But something in my reading or the arguments I heard had already convinced me I didn't want my twenty-five cents to be used to challenge other people's beliefs and cultures. I began leaving the missions side of my donation envelope empty. The minister's wife questioned this choice, prompting an angry defense on my part, and then my exit. And that was the end of my relationship with organized religion. I could not have imagined that so many years later I would witness liberation theology sweep across a continent, or be thinking and writing about religion and revolution.

Many years past that, already in middle age, I was able to remember as a child having been sexually abused by my maternal grandparents. My grandfather was a Christian Science practitioner, considered a holy man in our family. So I am also much too familiar with the extreme perversion many religious figures hide. In this sense I am sure my family history also facilitated my later aversion to institutionalized religion. My grandparents on both sides were Jews, but my maternal grandmother and grandfather hid their origins and passed their distaste (read: fear) on to my mother.

Religion wasn't insistently present in my childhood. Later, on my own, I briefly chose to participate. Then, for many years, I walked in another direction. During my time in Nicaragua, I became intrigued with liberation theology; its concern for the poor dovetailed with my developing political consciousness. I wrote a book called *Christians in the Nicaraguan Revolution*,[4] and long past the research for that book continued attending Sunday mass at a liberation theology church in Managua. The atmosphere at that church often seemed more conducive to open discussion of current affairs than did the more dogmatic political circles I inhabited.

Most religions hold up values of love and compassion, but hierarchy is paramount, and there is always a pope, patriarch, priest, pastor, imam, lama, rabbi, or guru at the top of the pyramid. Revolutionary movements also have their charismatic leaders. Typically, with few exceptions, political as well as religious leaders are men. Common sense would suppose shared decision making, so that if one person falls there are others to take his or her place; but history has shown that after a first brilliant figure dies, grows old, or falls from grace, those who follow frequently dilute or corrupt the message. We need only look to the Soviet Union or, more recently, South Africa. Since Che's life and death, a feminist analysis of power has allowed us to take a new look at these top-down strategies—either of belief or for instigating social change. It is not coincidental that attitudes of masculine dominance are so prominent in both arenas.

Revolution's goal is a better life for everyone. The people are supposed to be in charge. The health and durability of profound social change depend, in fact, on the degree to which those who lead a revolutionary experiment are willing to share power. In addition to the problem of diminishing morality among subsequent leadership figures, we have many examples of revolutionary strongmen who refuse to cede their positions, clinging to them for life. This causes a stagnation that subverts the health of a system. It is no more or less than power abuse.

So while religion and revolution—a new value system, blind obedience, and symbols strong enough to keep great masses of people within the fold—may be similar, their objectives are very different. This complicates an analogy that, in any case, I believe has merit. It may be an issue of deconstructing form and content, of understanding where they become one and where and how they fragment into separate entities, like cancerous cells growing wild and finally overcoming the healthy body.

There was one brief parenthesis of time in which the Catholicism so popular in Latin America breached the shackles of organized religion and embraced the pain, misery, and hope of people's lives. Liberation theology, what progressive Catholics call Jesus's preferential option for the poor, first gained prominence in 1962 during Pope John XXIII's Second Vatican Council. This Gospel-oriented Christianity achieved Latin American relevance at the 1968 meeting of bishops in Medellín, Colombia. Great numbers of believers began to realize that there didn't have to be a contradiction between faith and revolution. It is worth noting that these two dates perfectly bracket Che's death in Bolivia. Then it wasn't just the image of the dead guerrilla who typified a Christ freed from repressive religious dogma; the Colombian priest turned guerrilla fighter Camilo Torres, Archbishop Oscar Romero in El Salvador, and others began appearing in popular iconography, brilliant halos circling their heads and a rifle or political sermon replacing the cross or shepherd's staff.

In other important battles, too, there have been moments in which organized religion has retrieved its roots and pushed past the institutional strictures that have kept it in the oppressor camp. During the US civil rights movement the black churches were important centers of struggle. Quakers set an example when they provided humanitarian aid to both sides during the US war in Vietnam. Buddhists played a vital role during that war as well, and they continue to do so in the campaign for the liberation of Tibet. In general, though, religion walks a path that is patriarchal, dogmatic, and controlling. Revolution is immeasurably weakened when it follows that same path.

Discussions about art imitating life and life imitating art have raged in various contexts in recent years. Che's life and death, in all their contradictions and dramatic revelations, certainly inspire a great deal of art. But life also imitates the art Ernesto Guevara created simply by living and dying the way he did. There is a dialectical movement here, one in which I often feel I am dancing in slow motion with legacy. In my mind, in my memory, and on my body, life and art imitate each other.

Aleida March and Che Guevara, political rally.
Cuba, 1960. Photographer unknown.

chapter fifteen
che's legacy for today's activists

I've talked about the lasting power of Che's image—in art and on every imaginable pop culture item in our commodity-oriented societies. It is an image that rivals the crucified Christ and the Buddha seated in meditation. And—like these—its power and meaning are as diverse as the young men or women who continue to stencil it on a wall or wear it on a T-shirt.

Each new generation of rebels or nonconformists claims Che's symbol for itself. His image is known not only among serious progressive people committed to changing society but also among many others, including extremists whose actions we find appalling. For those like myself, who remember our activist days with nostalgia, it has become something familiar and intimate, reminding us of more hopeful times.

Beyond the symbol, we might ask ourselves what Che's legacy really means for today's activists and the millions of others who sport his image. For the second group, those on every continent who wear a shirt with the familiar beret-topped face but may know little or nothing about the man behind the image, it probably represents some vague sense of rebellion and courage, maybe denoting nothing more than a purely macho stance. It is likely also a statement against social hypocrisy in a world in which power suffocates and demeans.

I am most interested in exploring what Guevara the man has bequeathed in terms of useful legacy for today's more conscious rebels: those on the front lines of the demonstrations against the World Trade Organization (WTO); those who demonstrate against nuclear proliferation or imperialistic war; those who raise consciousness about global warming and climate change; those who lash out at the corporate mega-magnates who continue to orchestrate an economic crisis that has made them billions while robbing so many of homes and livelihoods; those who populate the Occupy encampments across the United States or take part in similar movements sweeping Europe, Latin America, and other parts of the world; even those who, individually and in less public ways, write or sing or paint their dreams of a different world.

Can we still learn from Che's example? If so, what? And how?

Che was a natural leader, a man whose background, education, and travels prepared him well for the life he chose. A great deal has been written about his leadership qualities; I have referenced some of that here. During the Cuban campaign, Che's conduct won him admiration from all sides. And after the war, he continued to display the courage of his convictions, defending those convictions even when they conflicted with the Cuban Communist Party line. By the end of the war he had achieved the rank of *comandante*, the highest in the new military structure, and in peacetime he was named director of the national bank and then minister of industry. He was the only foreigner to occupy such pivotal posts.

In the subsequent military campaigns with which he was involved on far-off battlefronts, Che insisted on maintaining a leadership role. In Congo, he was forced to defer to his hosts; his white skin, ignorance of and alienation from local customs, and disgust at what he considered primitive beliefs and poor guerrilla tactics led to his withdrawing with a sense of personal failure. In Bolivia, strategic differences and the fact that the secretary general

of the Bolivian Communist Party demanded control of the guerrillas created insoluble problems. Che refused to give in. It wasn't
an option he even considered. We can trace a history of verticality.

Many of Che's innate leadership qualities continue to be relevant. But a number of groups working for social change today re-
ject this idea of top-down authority. They have seen individual
brilliance morph into something more devious and convoluted,
the lust for control leading to a single figure—most often male—
or small group of men becoming entrenched and holding onto
power far too long. The more experienced among them know this
model can betray and destroy movements, profoundly affecting
and grossly distorting the new social relations for which they sacrifice so much. Some are experimenting with more horizontal and/
or egalitarian structures, although to date spontaneous efforts such
as the Occupy movement haven't really come up with a viable or-
ganizational alternative.

Let's look at Che's military strategy. Except in rare instances,
the *foco* theory would be unimaginable in today's world. Globalization, the immediacy of information exchange, the volatility
of the financial markets, the impunity with which imperialistic
wars are fought, and the weaponry used in them have changed
the parameters of struggle. Today we confront a culture of multi-
national corporations, military and intelligence organizations that
easily work across borders, and national and international interests that are so tightly intertwined as to confound the most experienced opposition.

The Mexican Zapatistas may be unique in successfully developing an alternative model, but their indigenous culture and the fact
that state power is not their immediate goal have so far made them
an intriguing exception rather than an example to be followed. We
must also consider that leadership in war necessarily differs from
leadership in the construction of a new society. Even the Zapatistas employed a more military model during their initial rebellion
in 1994. Although we now understand that leadership problems

during the armed struggle phase of revolutionary change affect the ways in which power is distributed later, it is not yet clear how hierarchical discipline during the war itself can be squared with a more democratic model once victory has been achieved.

I have stated elsewhere that I believe one of the primary reasons we twentieth-century political activists failed in our efforts to change society was that we weren't able to prioritize an analysis of power: cross-class, cross-gender, and across the division between vanguard and masses. This led to a vanguardist approach, inevitably creating a distance between leaders and various oppressed groups, as well as causing many who initially supported the struggle to lose confidence in their leaders. I have not yet seen a model of horizontal discussion and decision making that has worked in any major political venue. I do, however, know that the old authoritarian model cannot lead to enduring change.

From the failed battles of the 1960s through the 1980s, at least some have learned that the sort of change they envision must be woven into the struggle itself; no longer is the promise "There will be plenty of time for that later" one that satisfies. In this respect as well, Che's too often unilateral and male-centered action is no longer considered a recipe to be followed, although, as I say, no one has yet come up with a viable substitute. In this respect, at least, Che's leadership style doesn't seem to provide a usable legacy.

Neither, I would argue, does the traditional Marxist worldview that formed the basis of the man's political education. Che proclaimed his communism from the moment he and Fidel Castro met in Mexico. He knew the important texts and had ideas about how their revolutionary theory might be applied in Latin America. Later he voiced his disagreement with the Soviet Union's implementation of Marxism, particularly in terms of the economy. Even at a time when the October Revolution was still in its glory days, he already understood its contradictions. As we have seen, he was more interested in what Mao was doing in China, and he looked to that country, with its agriculturally based economy, as a model that might have relevance for Cuba. Still, moving from capitalism to socialism was seen as the only way imperialist hegemony could be challenged and a different world established.

Gone are the days when Marx's ideas were taken as dogma or Lenin's theory of a ruling party was the gold standard in revolutionary currency. In fact, few of the traditionalist formulas put forth by any of the twentieth-century socialist countries seem viable to those intent on promoting social change today. Most of the old recipes have shown themselves to be problematic in one way or another, although there may also be a tendency to disregard what is important in Marx's analysis of capitalism or Lenin's vision of a vanguard party to the detriment of effective political analysis.

Marx's grasp of capitalist economics remains an important tool. Class struggle is still real, although increasingly more complex than it was in Marx's time. And most activists today believe that some form of organization is necessary to impose discipline and move the struggle forward. But many Left political thinkers factor a host of other contradictions into their view of society: race, gender, sexual identity, access to information technology, globalization, a hegemonic world, and the power that world has to coerce and manipulate through sophisticated advertising. There is the serious problem of climate change, the desperate need to develop sustainable energy, and a growing sense of agency in the global South. The collective good, while immensely important, no longer so flagrantly outweighs the rights of the individual. Both the eradication of poverty and individual freedoms of expression, discussion, protest, and movement are imperatives now (although we have yet to find ways of seamlessly meshing the personal with the social).

So if Che's roots in classical Marxism and the top-down leadership style for which he was known aren't appropriate to a new generation of social activists, what is his legacy? Have the T-shirts and coffee mugs become mere objects of a popular culture emptied of its original meaning? Is a young person who paints Che's name on a city wall somewhere in the world acting without understanding that for which the hero stood? Has some living connection been broken?

I don't think so.

As I said at the beginning of these musings, I believe Che's greatest legacy is his unerring capacity to unify words and action, to be who he said he was. His lack of hypocrisy and principled stand in every one of life's arenas are still uniquely worthy models. And in a world increasingly ruled by official deceit, they become ever more precious. Speaking only as a citizen of the United States, I can say that never have governmental doublespeak and double-cross at every level been more apparent than they are today. Never have the major corporations taken more blatant advantage of ordinary working people or, with the exception of a very few scapegoats, enjoyed such impunity. Never have our young people been asked to give their lives and sanity in such a stream of immoral, arrogant, illegal, and counterproductive wars. The current revival of American exceptionalism is both shocking and dangerous. The example of a man who sought justice and martyred himself to that end is powerful, if only because it shows there is an alternative to such machinations.

Che exemplified sacrifice. A simple reading of any of his several campaign diaries makes palpable the great personal sacrifices he endured, from leaving his wife and children to making his way across inhospitable landscapes in several foreign countries and enduring asthma attacks that would have defeated someone less determined. In peacetime, his refusal of privilege attests to his sense that sacrifice came with the territory; it was not something to be applauded but, rather, a quality he considered natural in the daily life of a principled human being. As long as this willingness to sacrifice is accompanied by a correct assessment of struggle and welcomes input from a variety of sources, it certainly continues to have relevance for today's activists.

Che stands for another value as well: the importance of independent study and ceaseless questioning. In his time, especially during his tenures at the head of Cuba's Ministry of Industry and national bank, he studied every industrial, agricultural, and political model he thought might have relevance for Cuba's transition to socialism. He constantly read in other disciplines as well, from literature and art to anthropology, mathematics, and physics. He was unorthodox in the extreme, refusing to accept party lines or whatever models were being put forth as automatic answers to a war-ravaged country struggling to emerge from underdevelopment. His conclusions often earned him criticism from whatever establishment enjoyed momentary favor, and as Cuba came more fully into the socialist bloc and was pressured to acquiesce to its program, he sometimes found himself defending unpopular positions. At such times the consistency between his ideas and actions was impressive, winning him admiration even from his enemies.

I think Che's passion to learn about everything from economics to medicine, from guerrilla warfare to agronomy and art, and his constantly questioning mind are valuable examples for today's social activists. We are tired of the follow-the-leader mentality that has so often led us blindfolded to disaster. We would do well to emulate someone who read widely, listened to others, discussed passionately, and usually had the wisdom to change his mind when that was warranted.

Today's activists have information and communication access undreamed of in Che's time. The Internet has made online activism not only possible but a powerful tool for young people today. A single posting can rally millions, to Tahrir Square or anywhere else. And we can see photos and videos of demonstrations ignored or trivialized in our corporate media. Needless to say, the Internet and its social media cut both ways: expert hacking can produce WikiLeaks, on the one hand, and profile every person's most intimate secrets, on the other. When Che lived, none of this technology existed. In Cuba radio *bembá* (gossip) carried the news in a matter of minutes. Che's own campaign diaries, with their carefully kept records of battles, troop morale, and other details, were as immediate as we had. In the Bolivian theater in particular, tapes and photographs left in places presumed safe played a tragic part in leading the enemy to the revolutionaries' whereabouts.

Internationalism is without a doubt one of Che's most important legacies, not only for today's social activists but for anyone concerned about our future and the future of our planet, anyone who hopes to contextualize their sense of self in the world. Extreme nationalism is one of our most dangerous ideologies, internationalism its surest remedy.

More than almost any other historical figure, Che embodied empathy for peoples everywhere and their plights. As I have shown, his strategy for internationalist struggle had its flaws, some of them serious. But the intention and constancy were there. He dedicated his life to bringing about social change, without thought to borders. And his life was cut short in that endeavor.

Che possessed a unique combination of creativity and discipline, qualities too often considered mutually exclusive. He showed us that creative thought and the determination to act on that thought can bring innovative results. He was also a paradigm of courage. Rarely has history given us someone with such courage of conviction, in action as well as ideas.

Che's legacy is more than the beautiful face and piercing gaze. It is much more than a history known very partially to the vast majority of those who cherish the symbolism of his name. It is relevant despite an increasing unfamiliarity with the man's ideals or the particular choices he made. Resistance, rebellion, the conviction that change is possible and hope lives: these are the qualities Che represents, in every culture and language.

Beyond academic inquiry or theoretical relevance, his is a rebel energy imprinted on generation after generation. In Che, the saint (in its secular iteration) and the outlaw (in its broadest definition) inhabit a single body. His image is relevant to any situation and personifies what is best in us all: nothing less than human dignity.

chapter sixteen
poetry closes the circle and
opens infinite circles

Che loved literature. He read it avidly in his youth, wrote some
rather bad poems and several interesting stories, and carried well-
worn collections in his backpack through all his military campaigns. In one of his Bolivian diary entries he mentioned reading as a privilege not shared by the rest of his troop and worried
it might set him apart in some negative way, making him seem
aloof. Yet he needed this nourishment and often carried a book
even when he didn't have the space for extra rations.

His taste was broad, including classical Greeks such as Pindar,
Aeschylus, Sophocles, Euripides, and Plato; Dante, Goethe, Cer-
vantes, and Shakespeare; and poets Walt Whitman, Antonio Ma-
chado, Federico García Lorca, León Felipe, Pablo Neruda, César
Vallejo, Rubén Martínez Villena, and Nicolás Guillén.

Hilda Gadea, writing about her life with Guevara in Guatemala
and Mexico, replays the many times he recited his favorite poems
to her. She mentions a number of women poets, among them the
Chilean Gabriela Mistral, the Argentinean Alfonsina Storni, and
Uruguayans Juana de Ibarborou and Sara de Ibáñez. Gadea said
that she introduced him to Ibáñez and that they both considered

The most iconic image of Che Guevara, taken at the memorial to the more than eighty victims of the Belgian transport *Coubre*, which exploded in Havana harbor as a result of counterrevolutionary sabotage. Havana, March 5, 1960. Photo by Alberto Díaz (Korda).

her the best postmodernist woman poet. She recalled that he recited José Hernández's long *Martín Fierro* to her from memory.[1]

Poets love Che. Thousands have written to and about him, before and after his death. Maybe it is to some of these poems I should go to look for the more subtle clues to his enduring power. And so I close with a nod to poetry: how it figured in Che's life and how Che remains present in the poetry of so many different languages.

In 1965, before Che's death but after he had gone on to other battlefields, Cuban poet Miguel Barnet wrote a brief poem titled only, as so many others have been, "Che":

> Che, you know it all,
> each nook and cranny of the Sierra,
> asthma in the cold grass,
> the speaker's rostrum,
> night tides
> and even
> how fruit grows, how oxen are yoked.
>
> I would not give you
> pen for pistol
> but you are the poet.[2]

The brief poem would be translated into many languages and, following Che's death, reproduced often. The poet acknowledges the man's asthma, a defining characteristic. Then, after recognizing his expertise in so many disparate fields, he makes it clear that his life itself is a poem and therefore he is the poet. In ten brief lines he says it all. This brings us back to Haydée Santamaría's farewell letter to Che — itself a poem — in which she comments on Fidel having bestowed upon him the rank of artist, the highest rank of all. Or to Che's important "Socialism and Man in Cuba," in which he devotes so much space to artistic creation in the building of a new society.

In his monumental "Conversations," the great Argentinean poet Juan Gelman—Guevara's contemporary—evoked the impact the man would have on others when he wrote, soon after Che's death:

> I am from a country where a short while ago Carlos Molina
> Uruguayan anarchist and minstrel
> was arrested
> in Bahía Bahía in the south of the South
> facing the immense sea as they say
> he was arrested by the police
> Carlos Molina was
> singing, spinning ballads
> about the vast ocean voyages
> the monsters of the vast ocean
> or ballads for example
> about the horse that lies down on the pampas
> or about the sky one supposed Carlos
> Molina was singing as ever beauties and sorrows when
> suddenly Che began to live and die in his guitar
> and so the police arrested him.[3]

Throughout Latin America, in the dark times leading up to and following the guerrilla leader's murder, mere evidence of Che's example in the lines of a song could result in serious repression. Portuguese poet Sophia de Mello also evoked the way the man's legacy lives on in those he influenced, but she did so out of her own national experience when she wrote "Che Guevara" in 1972. Here are the last six lines from that poem:

> From poster to poster your image decorates our
>   consumer society
> Like Christ in blood decorates the sponsored
>   alienation of churches
> However
> Before your face

The adolescent meditates in his room
When he seeks to emerge from a world that is rotting.[4]

Uruguayan Mario Benedetti's poem "In Grief and Rage," written in 1967 just after Che's death, begins:

So here we are
filled with grief
and rage
even if your death is
one more predictable absurd . . .[5]

The following year, Trappist monk Thomas Merton wrote from Kentucky with poignant familiarity: "I write letters to you, Che, / under poisoned rains."[6] His is an intimate conversation in which he confides his own deepest concerns to the monumental figure.

And Allen Ginsberg, from a different culture and in a very different tone, begins his 1967 "Elegy Che Guevara" by describing the dead hero as

European Trib. boy's face photo'd eyes opened,
young feminine beardless radiant kid
lain back smiling looking upward
Calm as if ladies' lips were kissing invisible parts of the body
Aged reposeful angelic boy corpse . . .[7]

Some might find Ginsberg's lines disrespectful, but that would be a narrow response. One of the most profound things about Che's image is that each of us receives it intimately, with a language that speaks to our deepest self.

The Spaniard Rafael Alberti, who had known the Guevara family before Ernesto became Che, wrote "To Ernesto Che Guevara" in 1970:

I met you as a boy
there in that countryside of Argentine Córdoba
playing among the poplars and maize fields,

the cows of the old manors, the peons. . . .
I did not see you again, until I learned one day
that you were the bloodstained light, the north,
that star
that has to be watched at every moment
so as to know where we stand.[8]

Writing this text, I have explored an extraordinary man in the passionate, often misunderstood context of his time and place. I have come to understand why both Che Guevara's persona, to the degree I can know it, and his myth have captivated me, periodically pulling me to revisit his words, ponder the many images by those who have photographed or painted him, and explore the volumes written about his presence among us.

But there are myths and myths, and not all of them draw me. The one that does is the one that we, who want what he wanted, have woven to perpetuate his message: a red-hot flare of fire, the belief that a world of justice is possible. Risk and commitment. Consistency and the determination to push that consistency as far as humanly possible. Sacrifice and eroticism. Like few others, Che lives in me, sustaining my hope and nurturing my creativity.

notes

chapter one

1. Korda, formerly of Cuban fashion fame and later Fidel's personal
photographer, isolated Che's face from the crowd, printed it, and kept it
on his darkroom wall. Through the years, he began giving it to friends.
Gian-Giacomo Feltrinelli, an Italian publisher, was responsible for the
image's broad dissemination. When Smirnoff vodka used it, Korda sued
and won a settlement of fifty thousand English pounds, which he donated
to the Cuban medical system. He was quoted as saying his photograph was
made without lucrative intention, and he didn't mind it being reproduced
in the context of revolutionary causes. He did not, however, want it to be
used to sell commercial products. Trisha Ziff, ed., *Che Guevara: Revolutionary and Icon* (New York: Abrams Image, 2006), 23–24.

2. Referencing Mark Behr, in an unpublished discussion of masculinity.

3. Along with Diego Rivera, José Clemente Orozco, and David Alfaro
Siqueiros, Tamayo was one of the great Mexican muralists.

4. Mexico's quintessential Day of the Dead is celebrated November 1
and 2, coinciding with the Catholic holidays All Saints' Day and All Souls'
Day. Festivities actually begin several days earlier. Families gather in grave-
yards and construct elaborate altars with photographs and food offerings
in private homes. November 1 is the day for honoring dead infants and
children, while November 2 honors deceased adults.

5. In 1987 Argentinean artist and filmmaker Leandro Katz began to
search for the photographer who had taken that final iconic picture of Che
dead. He followed a complicated trail until he found Freddy Alborta in La
Paz, and he was able to interview Alborta in 1993. "I had the impression
that I was photographing a Christ," Alborta remembered a quarter century
later. "It was not a cadaver that I was photographing but something . . .

extraordinary." Leandro Katz, *Los fantasmas de Nancahuazú / The Ghosts of Nancahuazú* (Buenos Aires: La lengua viperina, 2010), 211.

6. Guevara and the Cuban revolution had been behind the failed attempt by Argentinean Jorge Ricardo Masetti to establish a guerrilla base at Salta, northern Argentina, in 1962. Some thirty Argentineans and a number of experienced Cubans took part. They called their small force the People's Guerrilla Army (EGP). After a few unequal encounters they were decimated by the military, and Masetti's body was never found. April 21, 1964, is considered the date of his disappearance.

chapter two

1. Just a year and a half after the new government came to power, in June 1961, Fidel Castro met with a large group of artists and writers to listen to their concerns about intellectual freedom and reassure them of the revolution's support. The most frequently quoted phrase from this meeting was "Within the revolution, everything. Against the revolution, nothing," words that have been interpreted in conflicting ways. Less often quoted from Castro's talk that day is "We ask the artist to develop his creative effort to the maximum. We want to create ideal conditions for artistic creation . . . because the revolution means precisely more culture and more art."

2. From Guevara, "Socialism and Man in Cuba," addressed at length later in this book.

3. Guevara wrote a moving poem during his months in Mexico titled "La vieja María," to a poor woman dying of asthma in the hospital where he worked.

chapter three

1. Guevara, *Pasajes de la guerra revolucionario* (about the Cuban campaign); *The African Dream: The Diaries of the Revolutionary War in the Congo*; and *El Diario del Che en Bolivia*. These are three editions, two in Spanish and one in English, from among many that exist in both languages.

2. Pacho O'Donnell, *Che: La vida por un mundo mejor* (Mexico City: Plaza Janés, 2003).

3. Dariel (Benigno) Alarcón Ramírez, *Memorias de un soldado cubano* (Barcelona: Fabula Tusquets, 2003).

4. Training Mexican guerrillas was done in great secrecy, since Mexico was the only country on the continent that had relations with Cuba.

5. The *foco* theory proposed that a small guerrilla group, through just and caring relations with the population, could rally a force capable of developing into a victorious people's army. This theory had worked in Cuba, a country with very different conditions from those in Bolivia.

6. Régis Debray (Paris, 1940) studied under Louis Althusser and worked, among other jobs, as a professor of philosophy. In the 1960s he wrote *Revolution in the Revolution*, an analysis of the doctrines prevalent on the Latin American Left; the book became a companion piece to Che Guevara's manual on guerrilla warfare. Debray met with Che in Bolivia. He was captured in 1967, tried and sentenced to thirty years, but released after three. He held several posts in France's Mitterrand government. His main contribution to philosophical thought is mediology, a critical theory of the long-term transmission of cultural meaning in society. He has also written several autobiographical works, including one on his own experience in Bolivia.

7. Víctor Paz Estenssoro and his Nationalist Revolutionary Movement (MNR) made big changes in Bolivian life between 1952 and 1964. The most important included establishment of universal suffrage, nationalization of the tin mines, and a far-reaching agrarian reform. Miners organized effective unions, and peasants got access to their land. Although gains during this period continue to exist, the United States and local oligarchical forces weakened the revolutionary impetus, and the whole experience is sometimes referred to as the "unfinished revolution."

8. Although the official BCP did not support Che's guerrillas, some of its members quit the Party and joined the campaign. Complicating matters, a pro-Chinese split-off from the Moscow-oriented Party under the leadership of a man named Moisés Guevara also showed itself favorable to Che's guerrilla movement, but its support was mostly disastrous.

9. The Weather Underground was a radical Left organization that emerged on the US political scene in 1969 as a faction of Students for a Democratic Society (SDS). The Weather Underground's goal was to create a clandestine revolutionary party to overthrow the US government. It conducted a series of bombings through the mid-1970s, aimed at destroying important symbols of corporate greed and warmongering. These were always preceded by warnings aimed at sparing human life. After the war in Vietnam ended and the New Left in general declined, the Weather Underground remained the voice of a certain radical faction.

chapter four

1. Manuel Piñeiro Losada (1933–1998), sometimes called Barba Roja (Red Beard), headed Cuba's security apparatus. He was in charge of overseeing aid to guerrilla movements throughout Latin America. In midlife he married Marta Harnecker, a Chilean political scientist whose library of well-written pamphlets on political theory was required reading for Latin American revolutionaries of the 1970s and 1980s. Piñeiro died in an automobile accident in 1998.

2. Between April and November 1965, Che and an expeditionary force of more than one hundred Cuban guerrilla fighters answered Laurent Kabila's call for military aid in eastern Congo. Their presence there was a well-kept secret. Che ordered the Cubans' withdrawal when it became obvious to him that their involvement was a disaster.

chapter five

1. Carlos Quijano (born in 1900 in Montevideo, Uruguay; died in 1984 in Mexico City) was an important Latin American intellectual. He founded the weekly *Marcha* in 1939, and it ran uninterrupted until the Uruguayan military dictatorship shut it down in 1974. Quijano died in exile.

2. This and all subsequent passages in this chapter are from Guevara, "El socialismo y el hombre en Cuba" (Havana: Obra completa, Casa de las Américas, 1997).

3. I refer here to Salvadoran revolutionary and poet Roque Dalton, a close friend during our shared years in Cuba. Before Roque returned to El Salvador to participate in that country's armed struggle movement, we had many conversations, including some about woman's role in society. His posthumous book, *The Clandestine Poems*, contains the work of five imagined poets; one is a woman named Vilma Flores, whose work reflects some of what we discussed.

chapter six

1. Aleida March, *Evocación* (Mexico City: Espasa, 2008), 206–207, my translation.

2. Jon Lee Anderson, *Che* (New York: Grove, 1997). This quote was altered from the original, which stated that Lenin's NEP policy was started in 1924. Lenin died in 1924 and began NEP three years before his death in 1921.

3. Anderson, *Che*, 564–565, emphasis mine.

chapter seven

1. The *Granma* was the yacht that Fidel Castro and his movement in exile used to transport a troop of eighty-two men, including Che, from Mexico to Cuba. They set out from the port of Tuxpan, Veracruz, on the night of November 25, 1956. Bad weather, inexperience, and the poor condition of the boat itself caused delays, and they arrived on the Cuban coast wide of their mark and several days late. The voyagers disembarked on December 2, and Batista's soldiers were ready for them. About a dozen men managed to survive, disappear into the mountainous region of eastern Cuba, and initiate the war that two years later would bring the revolution to power. Che boarded the *Granma* as the guerrillas' doctor, but quickly traded his medical kit for a gun.

2. Hilda Gadea, *My Life with Che* (New York: Palgrave Macmillan, 2008).

3. Tania's real name was Haydée Tamara Bunke Bider.

4. Guevara, *La guerra de guerrillas* (New York: Ocean, 2006), 111, my translation.

5. Mark Behr, unpublished discussion of masculinity.

6. Audre Lorde, *Sister Outsider* (Freedom, California: Crossing Press, 1984), 53–54.

chapter eight

1. Ernesto Guevara Lynch, *Young Che* (New York: Vintage, 2008).

2. Colonel Jacobo Arbenz (1913–1971) was president of Guatemala from 1951 to 1954. He carried out land reform and other progressive measures. The United States, through its CIA, ousted Arbenz in 1954. He was exiled to Mexico, where he died in 1971. In May 2011, the Guatemalan government signed an agreement with his survivors to restore his legacy and publicly apologize for its role in the coup. The apology included a financial settlement to the family. Che was in Guatemala during the coup against Arbenz, and it profoundly marked his political development. He felt that the Guatemalan Left should have taken up arms against the perpetrators of the coup and that, had they done so, Arbenz would have been able to remain in power.

3. Guevara Lynch, *Young Che*, 225–226, my translation.

4. Gadea, *My Life with Che*, all passages from 30–36.

chapter nine

1. Fidel Castro, *Che* (Melbourne and New York: Ocean, 2006), 53–54.

chapter ten

1. Celia Hart, *Haydée del Moncada a Casa* (Buenos Aires: Nuestra América Editorial, 2005), 21, my translation.

2. Encrucijada, in the central Cuban province of Villa Clara.

3. Che's oldest daughter, Hildita, lived with her mother, Hilda Gadea. The four children he had with his second wife, Aleida March—Aleidita, Camilo, Celia, and Ernesto—lived with her.

4. Hart, *Haydée del Moncada a Casa*, 25, my translation.

5. Hart, *Haydée del Moncada a Casa*, 22, my translation.

6. The July 26, 1953, attack on the second largest military camp in Cuba was the action Fidel Castro and his men believed would spark the war of liberation. They chose the date because it coincided with the yearly carnival in Santiago de Cuba, a time of partying and drinking when they thought the dictator's soldiers would be sleeping off their good time. The action was a military failure but initiated the struggle that on January 1, 1959, would make Cuba the first socialist country in Latin America. Fidel's movement took the name "26th of July" in honor of the date.

7. After his death, Batista's torturers brought Haydée Abel's eyes in a basin. Whether this was an effort to make her talk or simply sadism for sadism's sake, who can say? She is said to have responded: "If you did this to him and he didn't talk, much less will I."

8. Hart, *Haydée del Moncada a Casa*, 26–28, my translation.

9. Silvia Gil, Ana Cecilia Ruiz Lim, and Chiki Salsamendi, *Destino, Haydée Santamaría* (Havana: Casa de las Américas, 2009), 103, 105, my translations.

10. Unpublished letter dated June 2, 1964, from Haydée Santamaría to Comandante Ernesto Guevara. Courtesy *Casa de las Américas*.

11. *Casa de las Américas*, no. 48 (January–February 1968): 3. This letter has been widely published throughout the world. None of the existing English translations satisfy me, so I have made my own.

12. Hart, *Haydée del Moncada a Casa*, 23–24, my translation.

chapter twelve

1. In the context of this continuity, it is interesting to note that Chato Peredo is currently a member of Evo Morales's government. Brothers Inti and Coco both died in the second stage of guerrilla warfare in Bolivia.

chapter thirteen

1. Bumiller, "West Point Is Divided on a War Doctrine's Fate," *New York Times*, May 27, 2012.

2. Peg Morton, *Feeling Light Within, I Walk: Tales, Adventures and Reflections of a Quaker Activist* (Eugene: Self-published, 2012), 286.

3. As I was writing this text, an Argentinean court convicted ex-president Jorge Rafael Videla, the dictator during that country's dirty war, for kidnapping the children of slain revolutionaries—only one of his many crimes. He received a sentence of fifty years.

4. This story is documented in the 2008 film *Pray the Devil Back to Hell*. To an important extent, the Liberian women's action ushered in an era in which women have been much more visible in African politics.

5. Cherie Zalaquett, *Chilenas en armas* (Santiago: Editorial Catalonia, 2009), 151, my translation.

chapter fourteen

1. There is some question as to whether Cuba is essentially Catholic. Many of the working poor have long been devotees of African Santería, while Catholicism has been more popular among the upper classes, great numbers of which left the country postrevolution. There is also a great deal of syncretism between Santería and Catholicism, with twin deities and a mix of beliefs. For several decades the Cuban Communist Party repressed religious sentiment and activity. Since it changed its policies in this regard, religious fervor has exploded in the arts. For the sake of what I discuss in this essay, I believe that Cuba—with some caveats—can be considered a Catholic country.

2. Marx, "Eighteenth Brumaire of Louis Bonaparte," second paragraph.

3. This image, by Cuban sculptor Enrique Avila, was unveiled on October 8, 1993. It is made of steel and reinforced concrete. A single line reproduces the image from the famous Alberto Korda photograph. To one side, also in metal and in Che's handwriting, is the quote "Hasta la victoria siempre" (Ever onward to victory).

4. Randall, *Christians in the Nicaraguan Revolution* (Vancouver, BC, Canada: New Star Books, 1983).

chapter sixteen

1. Gadea, *My Life with Che*, 52.

2. Miguel Barnet, "Che," *El Corno Emplumado / The Plumed Horn*, no. 19 (July 1966): 78, my translation.

3. Juan Gelman, fragment of "Conversaciones," in Gavin O'Toole and Georgina Jiménez, *Che in Verse* (Wiltshire: Aflame Books, 2007), 77, translation by Gavin O'Toole, used by permission of Juan Gelman.

4. Sofia de Mello, "Che Guevara," in O'Toole and Jiménez, *Che in Verse*, 230, translation by Richard Bartlett.

5. Mario Benedetti, "Consernados, rabiosos" ("In Grief and Rage"), in *Witness: The Selected Poems of Mario Benedetti*, trans. Louise B. Popkin (Buffalo: White Pine, 2012), 114–115, used by permission of the Mario Benedetti Foundation.

6. Thomas Merton, fragment of "Letters to Che: Canto bilingue," in *The Collected Poems of Thomas Merton* (New York: New Directions, 1977), 722.

7. Allen Ginsberg, fragment of "Elegy Che Guevara," in *The Fall of America* (San Francisco: City Lights, 1972), 70.

8. Rafael Alberti, "To Ernesto Che Guevara," in O'Toole and Jiménez, *Che in Verse*, 240, translation by Gavin O'Toole.

bibliography

Alarcón Ramírez, Dariel (Benigno). *Memorias de un soldado cubano*. Barcelona: Fabula Tusquets, 2003.

Anderson, Jon Lee. *Che*. New York: Grove, 1997.

Barnet, Miguel. "Che." *El Corno Emplumado / The Plumed Horn*, no. 19 (July 1966): 78.

Benedetti, Mario. *Witness: The Selected Poems of Mario Benedetti*. Translated by Louise B. Popkin. Buffalo: White Pine, 2012.

Casa de las Américas, no. 48 (January–February 1968).

Castañeda, Jorge G. *Compañero*. New York: Random House, 1998.

Castro, Fidel. *Che*. Melbourne and New York: Ocean, 2006.

Dalton, Roque. *The Clandestine Poems*. Willimantic, Connecticut: Curbstone Press, 1995.

Debray, Regis. *Revolution in the Revolution*. New York: Grove Press, 1967.

Echeverría, Mónica, and Carmen Castillo. *Santiago—Paris El vuelo de la memoria*. Santiago: Lom, 2002.

Gadea, Hilda. *My Life with Che*. New York: Palgrave Macmillan, 2008.

Gil, Silvia, Ana Cecilia Ruiz Lim, and Chiki Salsamendi. *Destino Haydée Santamaría*. Havana: Casa de las Américas, 2009.

Ginsberg, Allen. *The Fall of America*. San Francisco: City Lights, 1972.

Guevara, Ernesto Che. *The African Dream*. New York: Grove Press, 1999.

———. *El diario del Che en Bolivia*. New York: Ocean Sur, 2006.

———. *La guerra de guerrillas*. New York: Ocean, 2006.

———. *Manifesto* (with Rose Luxemburg, Karl Marx, and Friedrich Engels). New York: Ocean, 2005.

———. *The Motorcycle Diaries*. New York: Ocean, 2004.

———. *Pasajes de la guerra revolucionario*. New York: Ocean Sur, 2006.

————. "El socialismo y el hombre en Cuba." Obras Completas, Havana: Casa de las Américas, 1997.

Guevara Lynch, Ernesto. *Young Che*. New York: Vintage, 2008.

Hart, Celia. *Haydée del Moncada a Casa*. Buenos Aires: Nuestra América Editorial, 2005.

Katz, Leandro. *Los fantasmas de Nancahuazú / The Ghosts of Nancahuazú*. Buenos Aires: La lengua viperina, 2010.

Kunzle, David. *Che Guevara: Icon, Myth and Message*. Los Angeles: UCLA Fowler Museum of Cultural History in collaboration with the Center for the Study of Political Graphics, 1997.

Lorde, Audre. *Sister Outsider*. Freedom, California: Crossing Press, 1984.

March, Aleida. *Evocación*. Mexico City: Espasa, 2008.

Marx, Karl, "The Eighteenth Brumaire of Louis Bonaparte." In *Early Writings*. Translated by Rodney Livingstone. London: Penguin Classics, 1992.

Merton, Thomas. *The Collected Poems of Thomas Merton*. New York: New Directions, 1977.

Morton, Peg. *Feeling Light Within, I Walk: Tales, Adventures and Reflections of a Quaker Activist*. Eugene: Self-published, 2012.

O'Donnell, Pacho. *Che: La vida por un mundo mejor*. Mexico City: Plaza Janés, 2003.

O'Toole, Gavin, and Georgina Jiménez. *Che in Verse*. Wiltshire: Aflame Books, 2007.

Taibo, Paco Ignacio II, Froilán Escobar, and Félix Guerra. *El año en que estuvimos en ninguna parte*. Buenos Aires: Ediciones del Pensamiento Nacional, 1994.

Zalaquett, Cherie. *Chilenas en armas*. Santiago: Editorial Catalonia, 2009.

Ziff, Trisha, ed. *Che Guevara: Revolutionary and Icon*. New York: Abrams Image, 2006.